From MESS to MIRACLE

AND OTHER SERMONS BY

WILLIAM WATLEY

From
MESS
to
MIRACLE

AND OTHER SERMONS BY

WILLIAM WATLEY

Judson Press® Valley Forge

FROM MESS TO MIRACLE . . . AND OTHER SERMONS BY WILLIAM WATLEY

Copyright © 1989
Judson Press, Valley Forge, PA   19482-0851

Unless otherwise indicated, Bible quotations in this volume are from the Revised Standard Version of the Bible, copyrighted 1946, 1952, © 1971, 1973, by the Division of Christian Education of the National Council of the Churches of Christ in the U.S.A., and used by permission.

Other quotations of the Bible are from *The Holy Bible,* King James Version.

Library of Congress Cataloging-in-Publication Data
Watley, William D.
    From mess to miracle— : and other sermons by William Watley /
William D. Watley.
       p.   cm.
    Includes bibliographical references.
    ISBN 0-8170-1154-4 : $8.95
    1. Bible—Biography—Sermons.   2. Baptists—Sermons.   3. Sermons,
American.   I. Title.
BS571.5.W37   1989
252'.0783—dc20   89-36218
                                                                        CIP

The name JUDSON PRESS is registered as a trademark in the U.S. Patent Office.
Printed in the U.S.A.

In tribute to
The Rev. Matthew Allen Watley
July 1927–May 1987

Servant of God, well done!
Rest from thy loved employ;
The battle fought, the victory won,
Enter thy Master's joy. [1]

[1]Words by James Montgomery.

Contents

Introduction

Much of the truth of the Bible, both in terms of didache and kerygma, comes to us in the form of biography. Much of what the Bible teaches comes alive for us as we observe the triumphs and failures, struggles and conquests of the men and women whose faith journeys are recorded in Scripture. As we read the stories of women and men who are of like passions as we, both our worst and our best selves can be seen. As we read of their sufferings, trials, temptations, sins, faith, courage, and endurance, we sit where they sat. We weep with them, feel their pain, know their remorse, are touched by their compassion, and are inspired by their witness. Through their lives we learn the meaning of faith, love, grace, salvation, judgment, mercy, forgiveness, justice, stewardship, and prayer. Through their interaction with God we learn something about the nature of God's interaction with us. When we look at the women and men of the Bible, we learn how human beings, created by God from the dust of the earth, are redeemed by Christ and sanctified by the Holy Spirit, to the end that they live eternally among the angels in heavenly places. This book focuses on a few of those lives found in Scriptures who still speak to us about God's love and human potential.

There are a number of persons whose contributions I wish to acknowledge. First, let me again express my gratitude to God for Muriel, my faithful and loving companion for twenty-one years. When one has a wife who loves the Lord and has strong faith commitments, one's ability to minister to the people of God is immeasurably enhanced. My children, Jennifer and Matthew, in their own unique ways affirm the ministry into which they were born, support their Dad, and continue to make him proud.

My sister and friend, Mrs. Carolyn Scavella, has faithfully served as the first reader and redactor for all my books. Her sensitivity, perspective, and insights are appreciated. I also continue to be grateful to her husband and my friend, Donald, whose tolerance and sense of humor adds much to our sometimes heated discussions.

I am grateful to my administrative assistant, Rev. Marie Russell, who typed every word of the manuscript. Those who are familiar with my script know that her contribution was indeed significant. I praise God for the people of St. James AME Church in Newark, New Jersey. They listen to the sermons that are not of publishing quality as well as those that are! Serving them is true joy.

Since my last publication, my father, the Rev. Matthew A. Watley, to whom I dedicated my first book of sermons, has gone home to be with the Lord. Much of what I am as a shepherd and as a preacher, I owe to him. I am grateful that I had a chance to tell him so while he lived. If anyone who reads this book is helped in any way to proclaim God's Word more effectively or live the faith more dynamically, then the ministry of Matthew Allen Watley, servant of God and preacher of the Word, will continue to bear fruit.

Last, but certainly not least, I am grateful to my praying mother, Mrs. Marian P. Watley, a "classy" Christian lady, whom I have come to know in a new way since my father's death. Her strength, caring spirit, warm personality, gracious smile, and pleasant disposition have been instructive and an inspiration to all of us. From her we have learned how one bears one's sorrow with Christian grace and dignity.

William D. Watley
Newark, New Jersey

1

Less Than Dirt but Equal with Angels

Text: Luke 20:34–36
Supporting Scripture: Genesis 2:7

The words of our text were spoken in response to a question that had been posed by the Sadducees to the Master concerning the resurrection. I find it especially interesting that the Sadducees questioned Jesus about the resurrection since they did not believe in it. I have found that many people love to ask questions about religion for argument's sake. Since they don't believe, their questions are not intended to give more understanding of religion, faith, or the Bible. They want to argue, or they want to ascertain if we can defend our faith or if they can confuse us.

In ancient Israel widows were not generally allowed to inherit property. According to the old levirate law, if a man died childless, his brother was to marry the widow. If a child was born of this union, it would be regarded as the deceased brother's child and could inherit whatever property or estate had been left. The Sadducees posed a hypothetical situation to Jesus: Suppose a man died without child and his brother married the widow. The brother also died before the woman conceived. A third brother married the widow and also died before a child was born. In total, seven brothers married her, and all seven died leaving no offspring. Finally, according to the scenario, the woman died also. The Sadducees' question was this: Whose wife would the woman be in the resurrection?

Jesus reminded the Sadducees that if they knew the Scriptures, then they would not have to ask that question. Sometimes we must remind people who want to argue that they really don't know the Scriptures. They may know how to lift verses out of context and quote from the Scriptures, but they really don't know what they're talking about. Being able to memorize and quote Scripture is one thing; understanding the meaning of what is being quoted is quite another. Jesus told the Sadducees that if they really knew and understood the Scriptures with which they were trying to entrap him, they would understand that heaven is not earth. One cannot take earthly logic and conceptions into heavenly places.

Heaven and earth are two different realities, each with its own understanding of time, physical laws, and relationships. On earth, where death cuts off life and companionship, marriage is ordained of God for purposes of companionship and the propagation of the species. However, where death is no more and where we live in the eternal presence of God, which far surpasses any human relationship that we could ever have or imagine having, we neither marry nor are we given in marriage. Rather, as the children of God, as children of the resurrection, we live as do the angels and achieve equality with them, enjoying the same rights and privileges.

Salvation does more than save us from sin; it saves us to a new life whose eternal dimension ranks equal with the angels. The privilege of frail, poor, dying sinners, who have been redeemed by the precious blood of Jesus and are ranked with celestial beings who have never sinned, shows how great and dramatic and far-reaching is the work of salvation. To bring us to the place where we can exist in a relationship of equality with angels, God had to bring us a "mighty long ways."

When we read our supporting Scripture in the Book of Genesis, we are informed that God formed us out of the dust of the ground and blew into us the breath of life, and we became living souls. The Bible is very precise in its language; it does not mince words or use them casually. Rather, it says exactly what it intends. The Bible precisely states that we are formed from dust. Whenever the Bible refers to us, the word "dust" is used. God told Adam after the fall from innocence, "dust thou art, and unto dust shalt thou return" (Genesis 3:19b, KJV). The prophet Jehu, delivering God's Word to Baasha, said, "Forasmuch as I exalted thee out of the dust, and made thee prince over my people Israel . . . " (1 Kings 18:2, KJV). Job in his distress cried out, "Wilt thou bring me into dust again?" (Job 10:9 KJV). The psalmist has said that "He knoweth our frame; he remembereth that we are dust" (Psalms 103:14, KJV). According to the Scriptures then, we were not formed from the soil, or the ground, or the earth itself, but from its dust. As we all know, there is a difference between dirt and dust.

Dirt has body and can be gathered up with a shovel or held in one's hand. Dirt has properties and is so rich in nutrients that when seeds are planted in it, they grow. Because dirt has substance, it forms a foundation under our feet. Dust, however, is a different matter. Dust is the residue, the leavings, the waste of the earth; and as such it is less than dirt. Dust has no body and is virtually impossible to hold. It is so light that it flies into the air whenever we try to gather it up. Many times when we dust furniture, we scatter as much as we wipe away. And what does it do after it has been carried through the air? It either settles down on the same piece of furniture that we just cleaned or lands on another piece, dirtying it also.

Dust has no properties to make anything grow. We don't plant anything in the dust and expect it to grow. Dust does not have enough substance to serve as a foundation. Dust for the most part is useless, and its only real characteristic is its ability to cling and be carried through the air, which is what makes it a nuisance. Anyone who has ever tried to keep a house clean knows what a nuisance dust can be. For everybody's house, no matter how clean or neat it is, no matter how new or modern, has some dust. If we go into a new housing development and walk through a display home, we will note that those models are kept spic and span, picture perfect, but if we look carefully enough, we will see some dust. We can make a bed, and if no one gets into it, the bed will stay made. Wash a dish, and if no one uses it, the dish will stay clean. Wax a floor, and if no one walks on it or spills anything on it, it will stay shiny. But if we dust a piece of furniture, walk away from it, and return to it in a few hours or days, dust will have settled on it again. We just can't keep a house dust-free. Open the windows or the doors, allowing air to come into the house, and what do we get—dust. Or close up the house, allowing no outside air to enter, and what do we get—dust.

One of the more interesting aspects of the creation is that when God was ready to make a human being—the crowning glory of the created order—when God was ready to make that creature who would be stamped with the very image of the divine, God made us out of dust. God did not scoop up a handful of rich red clay or good black soil, but God seemed to have scraped the earth and gathered up the residue—the dust—to make us. God did not gather any of the fiery splendor of the sun or any moonglow or any of the brightness of the stars to make us. God did not extract any of the fine mists of the clouds or any of the vitality of the deep seas to make us. No, God made us from the leftovers of the soul, the dust of the earth.

The physical illnesses that afflict us and the death that overtakes us are constant reminders that at best we are frail creatures. Even the strongest among us, the most beautiful among us, and the smartest among us are, at our most bare and essential selves, differing configurations of dust. And that's why none of us have any business looking down our noses or assuming a position of superiority over another because of differences of race, gender, education, background, or bank accounts, because we're all made out of the same dust. We all come from the same dust, and when this life is over, we shall return to the same dust. There will not be one dust for men and another for women or one dust for black and another for white or one dust for the rich and another for the poor. There will not be one dust for the old and another dust for the young or one dust for Methodists and another for Baptists or one dust for Catholics and another for Protestants or one dust for Jews and another for Palestinians. We are all returning to the same dust.

Economically, dust is not worth very much. Someone has estimated that "the average human body within its flesh-and-bone area has enough fat to make seven bars of soap, ten gallons of water, thirty to forty teaspoonsfuls of salt, sulphur enough to kill the fleas on a medium-size dog, . . . phosphorous enough to make twenty-two hundred match heads, lime enough to whitewash a small chicken coop, carbon enough to make nine thousand lead pencils"[1] —all of which totals about five or six dollars in value in drug or hardware stores. People are willing to spend a fortune to preserve health in a body worth less than five or six dollars. We do it because we understand that our worth cannot be measured by dollars and cents. For, if the Scriptures are clear about anything, it is that not only are we made from dust but that we are also worth much more than the dust from which we are made.

When we were made from the dust, God blew into us God's very breath, God's very image, God's spirit, which transformed us from lifeless dust into a living soul. It is God's spirit that makes the difference between our being less than dirt and our being fully human. Even in creation God was sending a message that we are more than mere dust. That's why the psalmist could write:

> When I consider the heavens, the work of thy fingers, the moon and the stars, which thou hast ordained; What is man, that thou art mindful of him? and the son of man, that thou

[1]*Robert G. Lee's Sourcebook of 500 Illustrations,* Grand Rapids, Michigan, Zondervan Publishing House, 1964.

visitest him? For thou hast made him a little lower than the angels, and hast crowned him with glory and honour. Thou madest him to have dominion over the works of thy hands; thou hast put all things under his feet (Psalm 8:3–6, KJV).

With the human being, what one sees is never all that one gets because of the divine dimension of God's spirit within. When God blew the breath of life into us, God was letting us know that we are more than the dust we are and that there is a greater destiny to which we are called. We can never allow Satan or anyone else to hold us back or hold us down. We are more than creatures of dust, and God has called us to greater destiny. We can never allow anyone to tell us that because we are black or an ethnic minority or a woman or poor or physically disabled that we should only expect to do so much or go so far. We must tell those persons who put a ceiling on their own aspirations (or have allowed others to do so and are now in the ceiling business themselves) that we are more than dust and that God has prepared a greater destiny for us.

Young people, when you go to a party or school or your friends' houses and are offered a cigarette or drugs or a drink, before you take that first drink or puff or snort, remember you are more than dust, and God calls you to a greater destiny. You are called, not to conform to this world, but to be transformed by the renewing of your mind that you may prove what is good and acceptable and the perfect will of God. When we become discouraged and feel like giving up, remember that nothing that is good ever comes easily and that we are more than dust and that God has called us to a greater destiny.

Whenever folk who are gossips themselves try to make us into gossips, whenever folk who are petty themselves try to make us petty, whenever folk who harbor ill will themselves try to make us harbor ill will towards others, whenever folk who are vindictive themselves try to make us vindictive, we must tell them, "Get thee behind me, Satan. You may be my best friend, colleague, co-worker, or member of my family, but get thee behind me. For God has called me to do more than think earthy, dusty thoughts and speak earthy, dusty language and have an earthy, dusty heart and spirit and mind. I am more than dust, and God has called me to a greater destiny."

The fact that we, who are creatures of dust and less than dirt, can be made equal with the angels shows just how much God can do with nothing. Whenever I listen to the melodic music of Beethoven, who, though deaf, wrote symphonies, I say to myself, "My God, what hast thou wrought with dust?" Whenever I read the works of Milton, who, though blind, wrote about paradise, I say to myself, "My God, what hast thou wrought with dust?" Whenever I go to New York City and look up at the towers of the World Trade Center and the Empire State Building or to Chicago and see the Sears Building and the John Hancock Building, I don't say, "Look at what man has done." I say, "My God, what hast thou wrought with dust?" When I made my first trip to Rome and looked at the breathtaking grandeur of Saint Peter's Basilica and walked into the Sistine Chapel and looked up at the ceiling that Michelangelo painted while lying on his back, I said, "My God, what hast thou wrought with dust?" Whenever I get on a plane or board a ship and think about the fact that something that heavy can fly through the air like a bird or glide through the water like a fish, I say to myself, "My God, what hast thou wrought with dust?"

When I think about the amount of knowledge that can be stored on a computer chip or hear of another medical advance, the latest transplant or the newest technique in laser surgery, I say to myself, "My God, what hast thou wrought with dust?" But most of all, when I think that we who are made from earth's residue can be redeemed and sanctified to the point that we can be made equal with the angels of glory, that we who have borne the image of the earth shall also bear the image of heaven, that not only am I a child of the dust, but through Jesus I am also a child of the resurrection and thus can be made equal to the angels and archangels, to Michael and Gabriel and the company of heaven, I can't help but say to myself, "My God, what hast thou wrought with dust?"

> Then sings my soul, my Saviour God to Thee:
> How great Thou art! How great Thou art!
>
> And when I think that God, His Son not sparing,
> Sent Him to die, I scarce can take it in;
> That on the cross, my burden gladly bearing,
> He bled and died to take away my sin;
>
> When Christ shall come with shout of acclamation
> And take me home, what joy shall fill my heart!
> Then I shall bow in humble adoration [as a creature
> of the dust but equal with the angels]
> And there proclaim, my God how great Thou art!
>
> Then sings my soul, my Saviour God, to Thee;
> How great Thou art! How great Thou art![1]

[1]"How Great Thou Art," © Copyright 1953 S K Hine. Assigned to Manna Music, Inc. Renewed 1981 by Manna Music, Inc., 25510 Avenue Stanford, Suite 101, Valencia, CA 91355. International copyright secured. All rights reserved. Used by permission.

2

The Dumbest People in the Bible: Esau

Text: Genesis 25:29–34

Esau, the oldest son of Isaac and Rebekah and brother to Jacob, will always be remembered as the man who sold his birthright for a bowl of soup. He was a person who made one of the dumbest personal decisions and one of the worst business deals in history. Despite this fact, Esau was not a total waste; he had some good qualities. Esau was a skilled and cunning hunter, and as such was not totally dumb. A certain amount of intelligence and ability is necessary to out-think animals in their native environment and capture them in their natural habitat. Thus, Esau was not totally dumb; he simply did some dumb things, made some dumb decisions, behaved dumbly in certain situations, and had some dumb priorities.

Let us never forget that while none of us are totally dumb, all of us have done, and as long as life lasts will continue to do, some dumb things. All of us have Esau's cunning and skill in some things and his stupidity in others. Some persons can make major personal and business decisions with relative ease and then go to a restaurant and have trouble deciding what to order from the menu. Many times the waiter or waitress will have gone around the table and gotten everyone's order and still have to wait for such a person to make up her or his mind.

Esau was not only a rugged outdoorsman and a hunter of great ability, he was also a gentle person. He was especially devoted to his aged father, Isaac. When Isaac was old and blind, Esau was gentle with him and responded to his needs. If Isaac wanted something to eat, it was Esau who would get it. Esau also had a forgiving spirit. He forgave Jacob, his younger brother, who twice defrauded him. First Jacob took advantage of Esau's physical hunger to secure his birthright. Then Jacob stole Esau's blessing from their father. After many years of estrangement, when Jacob came back home with much fear and trembling, Esau ran to meet him. Esau embraced Jacob, fell upon his neck, and kissed him. Evidently Esau, unlike a number of us, could not go on hating and loathing, even when he had been wronged.

His noble qualities notwithstanding, Esau is most known for his despising his birthright and being dumb enough to sell it for a bowl of soup. History never tells the whole story of who and what we are. It always picks out certain actions that it considers to be most important. Sometimes what history records as significant might be different from how we might want to be remembered. Therefore we must be careful about the way we live and what we do so that what history records will be what we want remembered. We would want a legacy of which we can be justly but humbly proud, one that will not cause our loved ones, our friends, our children, and their children to hang their heads in shame. We would want to leave a legacy of character that will not cause our names to be associated with sin. Esau, for all his good qualities, is remembered as the man who was dumb enough to sell his birthright for a bowl of soup.

Once after a strenuous day of hunting, Esau returned home famished and tired and found his brother cooking a pot of lentils. Esau walked over to the fire and asked his brother for some of the red pottage.

Jacob said, "Not so fast, my brother. First sell me your birthright."

Esau said, "What use is a birthright to me when I am about to starve to death?"

Jacob, who understood that promises made when the stomach is empty are easily forgotten when the stomach is full, told his brother, "Swear to me first."

Esau swore to the deal and sold his birthright to Jacob, who then fed him. The Scripture tell us, "Then Jacob gave Esau bread and pottage of lentils, and he ate and drank, and rose and went his way. Thus Esau despised his birthright."

This incident doesn't say much for the characters of either Esau or Jacob. After all, Jacob was not behaving as a true brother. If Jacob had been a true brother, he would have gladly fed Esau. True families share with one another; they don't exploit one another or hold back from one another or mistreat one another. There are many groups of people who bear the name of family and many persons whose association with us is identified by such titles as "mother" or "father," "son" or "daughter," "husband" or "wife," "sister" or "brother," "niece" or "nephew," "uncle" or "aunt" or "cousin." However, their true relationship is not that of family. In an hour of weakness, crisis, or trouble, when death or sickness occurs, true family doesn't gather around like buzzards seeking what they can get for themselves. True family doesn't try to take advantage of or profit from or exalt the weakness of other family members. Whether we are talking about immediate family, extended family, or church family, there are some things that true family members don't do to one another.

Jacob's conduct was not that of a brother, and he must bear the initial responsibility for this dubious transaction since it emanated from his own avariciousness. The final blame for the outcome, however, must rest with Esau's stupidity and shortsightedness. He did not have to accept Jacob's offer, anymore than we have to accept the offers that we receive. We may not have much control over propositions we receive, but we do have control over those we accept. We can blame others for making certain proposals, but we must blame ourselves for our decisions to participate. We must accept responsibility ourselves for whatever consequences accrue from our decisions. We can blame Jacob's greed for starting this matter, but we must blame Esau's stupidity for the way it ended.

To understand why Esau made such a bad bargain, we must look for a minute at what a birthright meant in ancient times. Esau and Jacob were fraternal twins. However, since Esau was born first, he was considered the eldest. The firstborn or eldest son of a household had certain birthrights. He received authority and honor and a double portion of his father's inheritance. The eldest son often acted as the priest of the family in offering sacrifices, and the priestly garb was kept for him. He also received a special blessing from the father. In this case, the blessing would have included the promise made by God to Abraham, which was passed from one generation to another.

If Esau had kept his birthright, through him, rather than Jacob, all the families of the earth would have been blessed. If Esau had kept his birthright, his descendants would have been as numerous as the stars in the heavens and the sands along the shores. If Esau had kept his birthright, his descendants would have inherited the land flowing with milk and honey. If Esau had kept his birthright, Joseph, Moses, Elijah, David, Esther, and other heroes and heroines of God's covenant people would have been among his descendants. If Esau had kept his birthright, even Jesus Christ, the incarnate Son of God, would have been one of his descendants. Esau, however, sold his birthright. And what did he receive in exchange for the birthright that held the key for unlocking the future salvation of humankind? What did he receive for the birthright that contained heaven and earth, time and eternity in its certain fulfillment? He received a bowl of soup. How dumb can one be?

Someone has said that if we hold a penny close enough to an eye it will block out the sun. A penny can in no way compare with the sun, and yet, if we hold it close enough to an eye, we will lose sight of the sun. How foolish it would be to forget about the sun and concentrate only on the penny. How foolish it would be to act as if the sun didn't exist because we were captivated by the penny. How foolish it would be to look at life from the perspective of a penny held too close and miss the sun, which, though far away, nourishes and warms our bodies and turns night to day. Yet that is precisely what Esau did. He was hungry and tired; all he could feel were hunger pangs, and all he could see was Jacob's pot of lentils. At that moment in his life, in that moment of weakness, a pot of soup seemed to be the most important thing in life. The bright promises of his birthright seemed far removed from the reality of the bowl of soup that was so close. Esau allowed the present moment of hunger and discomfort to block out the larger vision of life. He allowed a bowl of soup worth only a penny to block out the sunlight of God's covenant, which even then was being fulfilled in his midst.

We may criticize Esau's stupidity in being so shortsighted, but how many times have we allowed the inconvenience of the moment, the hunger pangs for immediate rewards or instant revenge, or the temptation and passion of the moment to block out the promise of a glorious future? How many time have we allowed a penny's worth of passion, a penny's worth of greed, a penny's worth of ego, or a penny's worth of anger to block out God's Word, which even then was shining upon us? God's Word turns our midnights of sorrow into high noons of peace and nourishes us with its wisdom while it warms us with its truth. It is possible to become so fixated with our present pain and inconveniences that we forget what the future holds. When we're hungry and tired, Jacob's pottage can look and smell so good that we have difficulty remembering the value of our birthright.

When those who have hurt us mistake our meekness for weakness, Jacob's pottage of fighting our own battles or handling things our own way can look and smell good.

When we have been lied to, Jacob's pottage of getting even or seeking revenge can look and smell good. When we have said no to sin but seem to be enjoying life less than those who have said yes, Jacob's pottage of temptation can look and smell good. When honesty and virtue do not seem to pay, Jacob's pottage of compromise or underhanded double dealing can look and smell good. When we have grown tired of making sacrifices, Jacob's pottage of immediate gratification can look and smell good.

When we are told that everybody is doing it and we desire to be part of the "in crowd," then we must think and behave in a certain way. No one wants to be an outsider; everyone wants to be accepted—thus, Jacob's pottage can look and smell good. When we are told to believe that one time won't hurt, Jacob's pottage can look and smell good. However, any time we live only for the present moment of folly, vengeance, or greed, without thought for the future, we are acting as dumbly as Esau. Anytime we allow God's gift of the sun to be blocked by cheap copper pennies, we're doing the same dumb thing as Esau—we're selling our birthright to heaven for a bowl of soup.

Don't be dumb like Esau. Be smart and hold on to your birthright. Jacob's soup may satisfy for the moment, but it doesn't last long. Esau ate Jacob's soup—he ate until he had had enough; he ate until he felt he could not possibly eat another morsel; and he went away satisfied. But the next morning he had a problem: he awoke hungry. It's dumb to sell out one's morals beliefs, dignity, integrity, self-respect, and salvation for that which satisfies only for a little while. If we hold on to our birthright as God's redeemed and blood-bought children, we will inherit that which satisfies and lasts throughout eternity. Jesus told the Samaritan woman at the well, "Every one who drinks of this water will thirst again, but whoever drinks of the water that I shall give him will never thirst; the water that I shall give him will become in him a spring of water welling up to eternal life" (John 4:13–14). He told a group of hungry men and women,

"I am the bread of life; he who comes to me shall not hunger, and he who believes in me shall never thirst" (John 6:35).

Therefore, be smart—hold on to your birthright, for we can receive a double portion of the inheritance. Jesus said, "In my Father's house are many mansions; if it were not so, I would have told you. I go to prepare a place for you" (John 14:2, KJV). Hold on to your birthright, for we have been given authority; Jesus said, "Whatever you bind on earth shall be bound in heaven, and whatever you loose on earth shall be loosed in heaven" (Matthew 18:18). Hold on to your birthright, for we have been endowed with honor. "You are a chosen race, a royal priesthood, a holy nation, God's own people" (1 Peter 2:9a). Hold on to your birthright, for we can act as priests on behalf of others, for "the effectual fervent prayer of a righteous man availeth much" (James 5:16b, KJV). Hold on to your birthright for we have a special blessing from God: "He who conquers shall have this heritage, and I will be his God and he shall be my son" (Revelation 21:7).

3

The Dumbest People in the Bible: Samson

Text: Judges 16:1–31

Brawn without brains and muscles without a mind are no good. Irrespective of how strong, big, or fierce we are, if we don't have a developed mind and a mighty spirit to complement our size, we are more vulnerable to both attack and defeat than we would ever imagine. This is one of the enduring lessons that we learn from studying the life of Samson, the mighty warrior of Israel. Samson's strength was such that he could rip apart a lion as easily as we tear up a piece of paper. Samson's strength was such that he could slay a thousand Philistines with the jawbone of an ass. Samson's strength was such that he could lift the whole gate to the city of Gaza out of the ground and walk five miles uphill with it on his back. Samson, before whom whole armies trembled, was captured because he was outthought rather than "outfought." Samson was a mighty fighting machine, but unfortunately he was not a mighty thinking machine. He may have had superior strength, but the Philistines had superior strategy.

More often than not, victory goes to the superior thinker or to the side that has the superior strategy. One can have all the advantages on one's side, but if one does not know how to use what one has to the best advantage, then one is still at a disadvantage. Superior strength was not the reason for the bulk of Israel's victories. Israel had superior strategy—they had God on their side to fight their battles. The key to Samson's strength was the reality of God on his side. Samson's strength did not come from any special weightlifting or exercise program; his strength came from God, and his life was to be consecrated to God for special purposes. This was the message that the angel of the Lord gave to Samson's mother. The angel told her that she would conceive and bear a son and that he would be a Nazirite to God from birth. A Nazirite was one whose life was set apart and dedicated to the Lord. The book of Numbers, chapter six, states three requirements for persons who were set apart as Nazirites: they had to abstain from wine and strong drink; their hair could not be cut; and they were to have no contact with the dead.

When one reads about the visitation of the angel to Samson's parents in the thirteenth chapter of the Book of Judges, one cannot help but be impressed by the genuine piety of this family. They never doubted God's words but even besought the Lord to send the angel a second time so that they could be taught just what they were supposed to do regarding the care and nurture of their child. When one views the humility and sincerity of Samson's mother and Manoah, his father, one knows that these two godly parents would raise their son according to God's Word.

At some point, however, Samson began to visit among the Philistines. According to the Scriptures, Samson went down to Timnah, a town in the tribe of Dan, which at that time was in the possession of the Philistines. Samson knew of the tensions and enmity that existed between the Philistines and the Israelites. He knew how the Philistines periodically raided the cities of Israel and oppressed its peoples. He knew that to visit Philistine territory was considered taboo by his parents and others who were loyal to Israel. There he was, one of their most popular heroes and leaders, fellowshiping, relaxing, and courting among the Philistines.

Why did Samson visit Philistine territory? Perhaps he was

curious about life among the Philistines. Having lived the strict life of a Nazirite, having been told since childhood the story of the angel's visit to his parents, having been taught that his life was consecrated for a special purpose, Samson perhaps became weary of his strict regimen and began to chafe under the burdensome responsibilities of leadership. Perhaps the Philistine women looked more appealing, the Philistine men looked stronger, and the Philistine lifestyle seemed more inviting and exciting. Perhaps Samson felt he had nothing to fear—he knew that he could physically take care of himself and handle any situation that arose or any opponent who attacked him. Whatever his reasoning, Samson went down to Timnah.

Let us not forget that when we go places we ought not go, we go down. When the grass starts looking greener in somebody else's yard, we are going down. When we start forsaking our upbringing and disregarding those people who truly care for us, we are going down. When we start risking all that we are for the sake of curiosity, we are going down. When we start believing that we are strong enough, mature enough, and experienced enough to handle everything that we will meet in Philistine territory, we are on our way down.

Samson began to visit Philistine territory. He went down to Timnah and ran into trouble the minute he set foot on Philistine soil—first from the animals and then from the people of the land. He subdued the lion and vanquished the multitude that attacked him. He became involved in an ill-fated marriage that cost the heartbreak and disappointment of his parents. He became involved in an ill-fated wager that cost the loyalty of his wife. He became involved in an ill-fated act of revenge that cost the lives of thirty innocent men. If there is any lesson that comes to us from the misfortunes of Samson, it is this: God's people must stay clear of Philistine territory. Young people, stay out of Philistine territory. Married people, stay out of Philistine territory. Church people, stay out of Philistine territory. Never forget that you have been saved to a different kind of life than that of the Philistines. I realize that there are times when a life that is obedient to God's Word and will may be tight—but it's also right. There is nothing but trouble ahead for those who go down to Philistine territory.

As Samson vanquished his foes and defeated his opposition, he showed himself to be a threat to the Philistines. They began to watch him closely. They were witnesses to his strength and sought to discover his weaknesses. Never forget that those whom the Philistines cannot control or conquer, they seek to destroy. The Philistines noted Samson's visit to a harlot in Gaza. Samson's foes were able to observe his every move because he was right in their midst—living like one of them, talking like one of them, behaving like one of them. Those who associate with Philistines soon begin to act like Philistines. If we associate with trash, we'll soon begin to act like trash, for we take on the shadings of our environment.

The Philistines observed Samson's affection for another woman of questionable repute whose name was Delilah. They contracted with her to ascertain the secret of Samson's strength. They said: "Entice him, and see wherein his great strength lies, and by what means we may overpower him, that we may bind him to subdue him; and we will each give you eleven hundred pieces of silver." It pays to keep some distance from Philistines because they will find a weakness with which to trap us. If we talk with them about anything or anybody, they won't repeat what *they* said, but they will tell everything that *we* said. If we do anything with them, they won't tell what *they* did, but they will spread the news about everything that *we* did. While Samson was flexing his muscles, the Philistines had worked their minds and come up with the Delilah plan.

Delilah began to wear Samson down gradually. She cuddled up to him one evening when the fire was burning low and the mood was mellow and said: "You know, darling, I've never asked you for much of anything. I've never tried to pry into your personal life, but there is something I want to know."

Samson said, "Sure, anything."

She said, "Tell me the secret of your strength."

Samson thought for a minute, and, not wanting to tell her the truth, said, "If you bind me with seven fresh bowstrings which have not been dried, then I shall become weak, and be like any other man."

Delilah said, "Fine, now sweetie, lie back and rest yourself for a few minutes." Delilah sent for seven fresh bowstrings and tied Samson with them while he slept. She was so sure of herself that she had some men hidden away in the house.

As they came forth, she cried out innocently, "The Philistines are upon you, Samson." He immediately jumped up and in so doing snapped the bowstrings.

A few days later Delilah said to Samson, "Darling, you ought to trust me and not mock me by telling me lies. Please tell me how you might be bound." Samson, still being leery, said, "If they bind me with new ropes that have not been used, then I shall become weak and be like any other man."

Delilah rocked him to sleep and then bound him with new ropes. His would-be captors were again hidden away in a room, and so Delilah yelled, "The Philistines are upon you, Samson." He immediately awoke and snapped the ropes as if they were thread.

A couple of weeks went by, and one day as they were finishing their meal, Delilah said to Samson, "Why do you continue to lie to me. Until now all you have done is mock me. Tell me how you might be bound." As he finished his drink, Samson said, "If you weave the seven locks of my head into the web of the loom and secure them with the pin, then I shall become weak and be like any other man."

Delilah told him to go and rest himself on the couch while she cleared off the table and she would soon join him. Samson again fell asleep while waiting for Delilah. So, while he slept, Delilah secured and pinned his hair and then cried out, "The Philistines are upon you, Samson."

He awoke and pulled the pin from the loom, his strength intact.

I have always been puzzled when reading this story as to

why Samson didn't catch on to what was happening and why he didn't question Delilah as to why she was so interested in discovering the secret of his strength. Samson did not have to be a great mental giant or genius to see a clearcut scenario emerging whenever he told her the secret of his strength. The next thing he knew, he would be awakened from his sleep and bound by whatever he had just revealed to Delilah. One could understand this happening once, but not three times. Once is a coincidence or a mistake; three times is deliberate. One would think that Samson would have become suspicious after the second time, and certainly after the third. But Samson was so involved with Delilah that he couldn't see the truth that was standing before him; he was so tangled in sin that he couldn't think straight. Sin will make fools out of us.

In this instance Samson was really being dumb. Sin will make us do dumb things, say dumb things, and think dumb things. Sin will make us take dumb chances and adopt dumb priorities. To return to a land and spend time among those who have brought us nothing but trouble is dumb. To go against one's Nazirite vows, to forsake holiness and righteousness and believe that one can keep one's strength, is dumb. To fail to connect repeated Philistine ambushes with the fact that one has made certain revelations to a certain person is dumb. To trust any person with the kind of trust that should be reserved only for God is dumb. To repeat: sin will make us do dumb things.

After asking directly, after using seduction and caresses, after cooking and doing everything else she could, Delilah tried tears and pouting. Day after day she would say to Samson, "How can you say you love me when you don't trust me, when your heart is not with me? How can I believe that you love me when you withhold the truth from me? Three times you have lied to me and mocked me when I sought the secret of your strength."

After two weeks of Delilah's incessant whining and pouting, Samson said, "All right, Delilah, have it your way. I'll tell you what you want to know if you'll just let me have a little peace and quiet." The Scriptures tell us that he told her "all his mind." He said, "A razor has never come upon my head; for I have been a Nazirite to God from my mother's womb. If I be shaved, then my strength will leave me, and I shall become weak, and be like any other man."

When Delilah saw that he had told her the truth this time, she sent for the lord of the Philistines and told them to come and bring the money with them. Then, while she rocked Samson to sleep with his head in her lap, she called for a barber to shave off his locks. Then she called out again, "The Philistines are upon you, Samson."

The Scriptures tell us that, "he awoke from his sleep, and said, 'I will go out as at other times, and shake myself free.' And he did not know that the LORD had left him" (Judges 16:20). Many an individual, after taking one drink too many, after smoking once too often, after gambling one dollar too much, after lying one time too often, after trampling on the feelings of one person too many, has said, "I will shake myself free as at other times." But the person doesn't know that the Lord has left him or her because that person has been lulled to sleep in the lap of sinful pleasure and addictive habits.

"The Philistines seized him and gouged out his eyes, and brought him down to Gaza, and bound him with bronze fetters; and he ground at the mill in the prison." What Samson started, Satan finished. Samson went down to Timnah looking for a little excitement to relieve the strictness of his upbringing. He went down to Timnah looking for relief from his responsibilities. He went down to Timnah in search of freedom from his vows to the Lord. However, he went past Timnah and ended up all the way down in Gaza— without his vision, without his freedom, without the noble calling and honor that God had bestowed upon him as a judge of Israel. He ended up all the way down in Gaza as a chained and blinded slave.

Joshua once told Israel, " . . . Choose this day whom you

will serve . . . as for me and my house, we will serve the
LORD" (Joshua 24:15). In this life we are going to serve something or somebody. Better to be bound to God's love than
chained to Satan degradation. Better to be working in the
place where God put us than at the treadmill of sin's destruction. Better to walk by faith, seeing only a step at a
time, than to be blinded by sin.

Poor Samson, alone and forsaken, only a shell of the man
he once was. But the Scriptures go on to tell us, "But the hair
of his head began to grow again after it had been shaved."
His hair was not permanently lost; and as he labored at the
mill in Gaza, it began to grow back. That's the story of
salvation, of God's grace, of heaven's redeeming love. Some
of us have been in our own Gaza grinding at the mill of
self-pity, unable to see how we are going to survive. We are
witnesses that what we thought we had lost forever will
come back to us. Faith may leave us for a while, but even
in Gaza after we've hit rock bottom, it can begin to grow
back. Hope can leave us for a while, but before we realize
it, hope begins to grow again. God's Spirit may leave us for
a while, but even as it leaves, it begins to return. The joy of
our salvation can leave us for a while, but even when we're
in Gaza, it can return.

One day the Philistines had a great feast in honor of their
false god Dagon, and the hall was packed from top to bottom. During the feast they called for old blind Samson that
they might make sport of him. Samson asked the boy who
was leading him to place him between the two middle pillars
that held up the house. Then he prayed, "O Lord GOD,
remember me, I pray thee, and strengthen me, I pray thee,
only this once, O God, that I may be avenged upon the
Philistnes for one of my two eyes." Then he grasped the two
pillars and said, "Let me die with the Philistines," and pulled
the house down upon them and himself.

Samson prayed for vengeance and perished with his enemies. We can be smarter than that. We can pray a prayer of
salvation and of faith. We can ask the Lord to remember and

grant us eternal glories. One day on a hill called Calvary, three men were executed on crosses. The thief on the left railed at the condemned man in the center saying: "Are you not the Christ? Save yourself and us!" But the thief on the right rebuked his counterpart on the left, saying, "Do you not fear God, since you are under the same sentence of condemnation? And we indeed justly; for we are receiving the due reward of our deeds; but this man has done nothing wrong." Then he turned to the man in the middle and said, "Jesus, remember me when you come into your kingdom." Our Lord told him, "Truly, I say to you, today you will be with me in Paradise" (Luke 23:39–43).

4

The Dumbest People in the Bible: Haman

Text: Esther 7:9-10

Haman will always be remembered as the man who was dumb enough to build the instrument of his own death. He built the gallows from which he himself was hung. Haman, of course, never intended to be hung from this scaffold, since he had built it for someone else's destruction. Initially his actions seemed wise, but the fullness of time proved them to be dumb. Haman's tragic acts of stupidity are recorded in the precious Old Testament book of Esther, which is one of the two books in the Bible named after women.

Haman was the chief minister of King Ahasuerus of Persia. The king evidently was particularly fond of Haman, since the monarch required all of his other princes and officials to bow before Haman. For some reason Mordecai, one of the court officials, refused to bow before Haman. Perhaps as a Jew, Mordecai believed that such acts of reverence belonged only to God. Perhaps Mordecai felt that Haman was undeserving of his obeisance, and since he could not bow in sincerity, he chose not to play the role of hypocrite and violate the dictates of his conscience and his integrity. There are times when the children of God cannot bow. We do not intend to be difficult or offensive; we just recognize that there are some people, things, and issues that are worthy of our commitment, loyalty time and energy, and some that are not. The Scriptures identify a number of times when God's people went against prevailing norms and majority opinion and refused to bow. Among the Israelites who journeyed from Egypt to Canaan, God's own were those who refused to bow to the golden calf. God told Elijah about seven thousand others in Israel who had not bowed knee to Baal. In the book of Daniel, Shadrach, Meshach, and Abednego refused to bow to Nebuchadnezzar's golden image. In the Gospels, Jesus refused to bow to Satan in the wilderness of Judea. In the New Testament church, Christians refused to worship Caesar.

Often the price of not bowing is persecution, anger, hatred, and misunderstanding. These were the prices that Mordecai paid for not bowing to Haman's ego as well as his office. When Haman personally observed Mordecai's refusal to bow, he became enraged. The rage turned into resentment, which turned into hatred, which ultimately turned into a plan to exterminate Mordecai and all of his people. If Mordecai was not bowing because he was a Jew, then there ought to be no Jews, Haman reasoned. They all should be eliminated. With one swoop Haman could rid himself of everyone in the kingdom who might be inclined to follow Mordecai's example.

Haman used his favored position of closeness to Ahasuerus and several half-truths to persuade the king to initiate a program to exterminate the Jews. Haman didn't identify whom he was talking about, but merely told the king that there were certain people in his kingdom who were different from the others, whose culture and customs were different, and whose ultimate allegiance was elsewhere. All of this was true, but Haman also added a lie—that they didn't respect the law or the king of the land. That's why half-truths are more dangerous than outright lies; they contain enough truth to be believed and enough falsehood to be destructive. Haman proposed that these people be destroyed and offered to pay the equivalent of twenty million dollars into the treasury to cover the cost of his program of genocide.

Not knowing who was involved, Ahasuerus agreed to Haman's program and issued a decree ordering the extermination. As news of the decree began to spread, Jews throughout the kingdom engaged in acts of fasting, prayer, lamentation, and deep mourning. Mordecai clothed himself in sack cloth and stood outside the palace—an action that caught the attention of Esther, the wife and queen of Ahasuerus. Esther was Mordecai's niece whom he had raised since childhood; Esther thus loved Mordecai as a father. It was Mordecai who had planned and directed her ascendance to the throne. And Esther herself was a Jew. Of course, Haman was unaware of all these interlocking relationships. We never know all the truth or all the facts or all that we should know when we make it our business to traffic in half-truths. When Haman hatched his plot, he was aiming primarily at Mordecai. He had no idea that his scheme would reach into the palace, into the king's very bedroom and heart, for Esther was highly respected as well as loved by the king.

Mordecai sent a message to Esther to intercede on behalf of her people. Esther was fearful at first because, according to the custom of that time, any person—whether man or woman, wife or servant—who entered the king's inner court uninvited faced the penalty of execution unless the king extended the golden scepter toward that person. Esther had not been called into the king for thirty days. Mordecai sent to Esther the message: "Think not that in the king's palace you will escape any more than all the other Jews. For if you keep silence at such a time as this, relief and deliverance will rise for the Jews from another quarter, but you and your father's house will perish. And who knows whether you have come to the kingdom for such a time as this" (Esther 4:13–14). Esther asked her uncle to join her in prayer and fasting and resolved, "I will go the king, though it is against the law; and if I perish, I perish."

At one time or another God's children must adopt an attitude that says, "I'm going to do what I have to do, and if I perish, I perish . . . I'm going to stand for right and speak the truth, and if I perish, I perish . . . I'm going to trust God to fight my battles; I'm going to claim the promises in God's Word; while others plot, I'm going to fast and pray, and if I perish, I perish!"

God was with Esther when she appeared before Ahasuerus, and he agreed to give her whatever she asked, up to half his kingdom. She only asked that he and Haman join her for dinner that evening. During dinner when Ahasuerus asked what she wanted, Esther asked them to join her for another private dinner the next day and at that time she would lay before him the matter that was upon her heart. Haman left the palace that evening feeling pretty good about himself. He had received two invitations from Queen Esther to dine privately with her and the king. Surely no prince in the land had more power or influence than he did. Nothing could stop his rise to power, and no one could prevent him from doing whatever he wanted to do.

As he left the palace, Haman saw Mordecai, who still refused to bow to him. (God's children may be down sometimes, and others may be up; but they still don't bow.) There was Haman, feeling proud of who he was, and there was Mordecai, whose very presence reminded Haman that his power could be withstood and his authority be defied. Haman went home that night and built a seventy-five-foot gallows on which he would personally hang Mordecai. He would show that Jew who was boss. Haman resolved that he would ask Ahasuerus for Modecai's life the very first thing in the morning. He would teach him a lesson for his insolence.

But while Haman was building his offense again Mordecai, heaven was building a defense for Mordecai. While the power of evil was at work through Haman to destroy Mordecai, the power of the Lord began to work through Ahasuerus to save Mordecai. The Spirit of the Lord wouldn't let the king sleep, and so Ahasuerus sent for his book of memorable deeds of the kingdom. While reading the record, he discovered that long ago Mordecai had exposed a plot on the king's life, and he had never been rewarded for what he had done. Thus, while Haman fell asleep plotting against Mordecai, Ahasuerus fell asleep with gratitude for Mordecai weighing upon his mind.

On the next morning both Haman and Ahasuerus rose excitedly from beds of slumber. One was excited about the prospect of destruction; the other was excited about the opportunity for praise. One was excited about the prospect of doing evil to somebody, while the other was excited about the prospect of doing good for somebody. One awoke with a grudge; the other awoke with gratitude. I'm glad that when others get up early to do evil, there is a Sovereign Ruler who reigns over them who is prepared to do good for us. When others rise to curse, the Sovereign Ruler is ready to bless. When others rise to defame and criticize, the Sovereign Ruler comes to glorify and praise. When others build their gallows to hang us, our Sovereign Ruler reads our names in the Book of Life and is prepared to reward us.

Haman arrived early at the palace to ask for Mordecai's life, but before he could say anything, the king asked, "What shall I do to honor someone who truly pleases me?"

Since Haman had twice been invited to dine privately with the king and queen, he assumed that the king was talking about him. Thus he said, "Bring out some of the royal robes that the king himself has worn, and the king's own horses, and the royal crown, and instruct one of the most noble princes to robe the man and lead him through the streets on the king's own horse, shouting before him, 'This is the way the king honors those who please him.' "

Ahasuerus said, "Excellent. Go get Mordecai, and I want you to do everything for him that you have just said." Haman did as he was instructed and went home humiliated and perplexed. As he was telling his wife and friends what had happened, the king's messenger arrived to escort him to Esther's banquet. During dinner Ahasuerus again asked Esther what she wanted. The noble queen asked only that her life and the life of her people be spared from destruction.

The king asked who would dare touch her or lay hands upon her people. Esther pointed to Haman and identified him as the enemy of her people. The king was so furious and upset that he left the hall in haste to collect his emotions, while Haman threw himself at Esther's feet to plead for mercy. He who had so arrogantly planned the destruction of a whole race of people to settle a personal grudge had the nerve to beg for mercy. He who used his power and position not for good, but for evil, begged for mercy. He who wanted to kill the uncle whom Esther loved as a father begged for mercy. He who lied and schemed begged for mercy.

Just as the king was returning, Haman fell in despair upon the couch where Queen Esther was reclining. King Ahasuerus thought that Haman was making advances toward the queen, and Haman's face was immediately covered with a death veil as an indication of his doom. Harbona, one of the king's aides, told the king that Haman had just built a seventy-five-foot gallows from which he had planned to hang that same Mordecai who had saved the king's life from assassins. Ahasuerus ordered that Haman be hung in his own courtyard from the very gallows that he had ordered built for someone else. Thus Haman hung from his own gallows; he hung in his own trap; he hung in his own pettiness; he hung in his own greed; he hung in his own ego; he hung in his own vindictiveness; he hung in his own half-truths; he hung through his own scheming.

Haman thought he was smart, but he was not smart after all. Haman could have been a great man, but he let a little thing like Mordecai's refusal to bow prevent him from enjoying the honor and glory he received from others. We're not smart when we allow little things to steal our joy and prevent us from enjoying the blessings of life. He could have used his power for good, but Haman chose to use his power to fight his own personal battles. Whenever we use great power and great opportunities for little purposes and selfish ends, we're not smart. When we don't care who we hurt as long as our ego is satisfied, we're not smart. Whenever we set a trap for somebody else, we're not smart, because those traps might trap us in the long run. Whenever we plan evil for somebody else, we're not smart, because that same evil will come back to us.

Don't be dumb like Haman; be smart like Mordecai and Esther, who knew that the Lord would make a way somehow. Mordecai didn't know how or when, where or through whom, but he knew that the Lord would raise a deliverer from somewhere. He knew enough of his people's history to know that whenever they were oppressed, God raised a deliverer. When they were oppressed in Egypt, God raised up Moses; and after Moses, Joshua; and after Joshua, Gideon; and after Gideon, Samson; and after Samson, Deborah. When they needed prophets, God gave them Samuel and Elijah. When they needed kings to break Philistine oppression, God gave them Saul and David. Mordecai just didn't believe that God had brought them that far to leave them. Be smart like Esther, who understood that God had placed her where she was, not for self, but for service—for such a time as that. Be smart like Mordecai and Esther who didn't have to lay a hand on their enemy. Instead they prayed and fasted. For the power of prayer is stronger than any plot conjured up by evil men or women.

> Fret not thyself because of evildoers, neither be thou envious against the workers of iniquity. For they shall soon be cut down like the grass, and wither as the green herb . . . .Commit thy way unto the LORD; trust also in him; and he shall bring it to pass. And he shall bring forth thy righteousness as the light, and thy judgment as the noonday. . . . I have seen the wicked in great power, and spreading himself like a green bay tree. Yet he passed away, and, lo, he was not: yea, I sought him, but he could not be found. . . . But the salvation of the righteous is of the LORD: he is their strength in the time of trouble. And the LORD shall help them, and deliver them: he shall deliver them from the wicked, and save them, because they trust in him (Psalm 37:1–2, 5–6, 35–36, 39–40, KJV).

5

The Dumbest People in the Bible: Ananias and Sapphira

Text: Acts 5:1–11

The story is told that once a portrait was being painted of Oliver Cromwell, the great British statesman. Mr. Cromwell had a number of disfiguring warts on his face. The painter, thinking to please Cromwell and present a more-perfect-than-life picture of the great man for immortality, omitted the warts from his portrait. When Cromwell saw the picture, he said, "Take it away, and paint me [as I am] warts and all." The Bible does not give us idealized portraits of people, events, situations, or even churches. The Bible states the truth as it is and paints the picture as it is—warts and all. Whether the subject is Abraham, father of the faithful; Moses, the greatest lawgiver; Elijah, greatest of the prophets; David, greatest of kings; Eve, the mother of life; Sarah, the mother of the faithful; John the Baptist, forerunner of Jesus; Mary, mother of Jesus; or the disciples, companions of Jesus—the Bible presents each of them as they actually were—warts and all.

Luke, in his narration of the life of the early church in the book of Acts, does not differ from the biblical tradition of truth and honesty in all things. When he describes the early church, he shows it in its totality—warts and all. The picture of the early church that Luke paints in the first chapters of Acts is the portrait of a church that was conscientious though imperfect. In chapter 1 we see Christ before his ascension, instructing the church to tarry in Jerusalem until endued with power from on high, and we see that church gathered in obedience to the command of Christ. Thus, the picture that we see in Acts 1 is that of a church that was obedient and faithful to the word and will of its Lord, even though it was perplexed. The church of Acts 1 gathered, not out of a sense of routine or duty, but in response to the promise of Christ. The church was looking for, waiting for, praying for, and expecting something special to happen in its midst.

Acts 2 tells of the Day of Pentecost and what happened to the church when it was baptized with the Holy Spirit. We see Peter preaching with boldness and three thousand souls being added to the kingdom. We see a church with members who held their possessions in common, with distribution being made to everyone based upon their need, not greed. Thus, the portrait of Acts 2 is that of a Spirit-filled, fire-baptized, and anointed people. We see a church which received that for which it prayed. We see a growing and caring church.

Acts 3 tells of the healing of a lame man by Peter and John as they went into the temple and of the resistance to their ministry by some of the authorities. Thus, the picture that we see in this chapter is one of a miracle-working church that was not so involved with worship or administration that it could not heed the cries of human need. We see a church that gave what it had; we see a church that didn't allow opposition to prevent it from serving the Lord.

Chapter 4 tells of the arrest and examination of Peter and John by the Sanhedrin and how these two unlearned fishermen, under the power of the Holy Spirit, spoke with such articulation that they were released. Thus, we have the portrait of a church defended and sustained by the Spirit in the face of attack. The portrait of Acts 1 through 4, then, is that of an obedient, expectant, Spirit-filled, growing, caring, dynamic, and protected church. Who wouldn't want to belong to a church like that? One could get the impression that in a church so powerful, with the Holy Spirit doing so much in its midst, nothing could possibly go wrong, and Satan could not possibly enter it. All the members who were associated with it must have been saved.

Yet when the curtain rises on chapter 5, we discover that even this idyllic church had warts. In spite of all that the Lord was doing in its midst, it still had its problems. Even in a church such as this, there were hypocrites. If that was the case of the church as it existed in the wake of Jesus' immediate ascension, in the residue of the baptism of the Holy Spirit, and in the presence of the apostles and others who were eyewitnesses of Jesus' life and work, it will be the case now. The church historically never has been and never will be perfect on this side of the judgment. People who run from church to church looking for the perfect preacher, the perfect choir, perfect officers, and perfect members are destined to run forever.

Are all churches the same? No, they are not! Some are more spiritual, more liberal, more mission-minded, and more stewardship-oriented than others. However, even when we find a church suitable for us, it still will not be perfect. It will be a church with "warts and all." And if we embrace it, we are going to have to embrace it "warts and all."

The church, and even the heavenly community, has always had warts. Jesus didn't have but twelve disciples, and there were warts among them. One wart betrayed him, another denied him on the night that he was being tried, and the others fled from him. God created the heavens and the earth, the angels and archangels, and even among them there was a wart named Lucifer.

Acts 5 informs us that, true to form, in spite of all that was happening within the church, there were warts in its midst. There have always been those dumb enough to believe that they could take advantage of God's church and the trusting nature of God's people, without giving an account of their actions. There have always been those dumb enough to believe that things done for show or with a spirit of competition or without a sincere heart will be blessed in the same way as those done in faith and without regard for praise. There have always been those dumb enough to believe that they were smarter than everyone else. There have always been those dumb enough to believe that they could outsmart the Holy Spirit. Ananias and Sapphira were just that dumb.

According to the Scriptures, Ananias and Sapphira decided to sell some land and donate the proceeds to the church. Before presenting the money to Peter, they chose to hold back a portion of their earnings for themselves. There was nothing wrong in their keeping either part or all of the proceeds or even the land itself. Their sin came from the fact that they pretended that the amount they gave was all they received. Their deed was not careless, but contrived; it was not an honest mistake. According to the Scriptures, Ananias conspired with his wife Sapphira to withhold part of the purchase price for themselves.

Ananias brought the remainder of the money, laid it at the feet of the apostles, and then stepped back and waited for the applause and words of commendation and praise from the church leaders for his generous gift. However, instead of applause, he heard a deafening silence that seemed to last for an eternity. Instead of a smile, he saw a wrinkle on Peter's brow and perhaps a tear in his eye. Instead of receiving looks of admiration, he saw icy stares in the eyes of the church leaders that must have sent chills down his spine as Peter asked, "Ananias, why has Satan filled your heart to lie to the Holy Spirit and to keep back part of the proceeds of the land? While it remained unsold, did it not remain your own? And after it was sold, was it not at your disposal? How is it that you have contrived this deed in your heart? You have not lied to men but to God."

When Ananias heard these words, he fell dead. Peter didn't cast any spell on him or curse him. He didn't even touch him. No lightning bolt struck him. Ananias, realizing that no one knew of the plan but his wife and knowing that she hadn't told, now understood that the only way that Peter could have known was through the Holy Spirit, which hears all, knows all, and sees all. Ananias was so convicted by the truth and condemned by his own conscience that he fell dead. The young men of the assembly wrapped up the lifeless physical shell of his being and carried him out and buried him.

About three hours later Sapphira arrived, not knowing what had happened. If she had been sensitive to anything at all beyond her own greed and ego, she should have been aware that something was wrong. The sense of jubilation that is present in the church when good stewardship has been exercised was absent. People looked at her and looked away in shame and fear. No one seemed to want to say much to her. Peter, upon seeing her, asked if she had sold the land for a certain amount. When she said yes, he asked, "How is it that you have agreed together to tempt the Spirit of the Lord? Hark, the feet of those that have buried your husband are at the door, and they will carry you out." And immediately she fell dead and was carried out and buried beside her husband.

Poor Ananias and Sapphira, dumb Ananias and Sapphira—their deaths were so unnecessary. Why did they do what they did? The verses immediately preceding this story may hold a clue:

> There was not a needy person among them, for as many as were possessors of lands or houses sold them, and brought the proceeds of what was sold and laid it at the apostles' feet; and distribution was made to each as any had need. Thus Joseph who was surnamed . . . Barnabas . . . sold a field which belonged to him, and brought the money and laid it at the apostles' feet (Acts 4: 34–37).

Perhaps Ananias and Sapphira took note of what others were doing and decided they wanted to do the same. They observed the praise that others received and decided they also wanted recognition. Perhaps some of their friends, or even some people they didn't like, had sold their land and contributed the money. Ananias and Sapphira weren't going to let their friends or their enemies outdo them.

Ananias and Sapphira were afflicted with the same disease that is causing a number of us grief, sending some of us to the poor house and still others to hell. That affliction is commonly referred to as "keeping up with the Joneses." We see someone somewhere doing something or getting something, and we decide that we are going to do the same thing or get the same thing, whether we can afford it or not, whether we really like it or want it or not. It's dumb whenever we live in competition with someone else. It's dumb when we spend our lives and expend our energies trying to keep up with or outdo someone else. Someone gets a new hat or dress, car or house, or a new companion, and we must have one. Admiration is one thing, but it's dumb to try to be what we're not.

If there is any one great lesson that we learn from Ananias and Sapphira, it is that we must be real and sincere in what we do. It isn't just what we give, but how sincere we are in what we give that brings the blessing. One day a woman approached Jesus with a flask of expensive ointment and poured it upon his head as an offering of thanksgiving and love. There were those standing around who criticized her for what she did. But Jesus, who read the sincerity of her heart, said, "Let her alone; why do you trouble her? She has done a beautiful thing . . . .She has done what she could; she has anointed my body beforehand for burying. And truly, I say to you, wherever the gospel is preached in the whole world, what she has done will be told in memory of her" (Mark 14: 6–9). It has been two thousand years since Jesus uttered those words, and we are still telling the story of the woman and her alabaster flask.

It isn't how much we give, but how sincere we are in our giving that Jesus notices. One day he stood near the temple treasury, observing people giving their tithes and offerings.

A woman timidly approached one of the collection bins, put in two pennies, and slipped away into the crowd. No one paid her any attention, but Jesus turned to the disciples and said that she had given more than anyone else. Whereas others had given out of their abundance, she had given her all. It has been two thousand years since that day, and we're still telling the story of the widow's mite.

It isn't how well we sing, but how sincere we are when we sing that will bring the Holy Spirit into the church. It's not how long we pray, but how sincerely we pray that will bring miracles from heaven. It's not how loudly we testify, but how sincere we are when we testify that will encourage the hearts of the saints. It isn't how well we preach, but how sincere we are when we preach that will bring souls into the kingdom.

My constant prayer for the church is that the Lord will keep us humble at the foot of the cross so that we will be real in what we do. I pray that whatever we do will not be for show, nor with a grudging spirit, but with joy because we are convicted, directed, and moved by the Holy Spirit. For the Holy Spirit is real—its work, judgment, comfort, and unction are real. I pray that we will be as real and sincere in what we do as the God who created us, the Jesus who saved us, and the Holy Spirit that breathes upon us. I pray that we will be as real as the love that sacrificed itself for our salvation, as real as the salvation that gives us hope of eternal life, as real as the heaven in our view.

6

The Dumbest of the Dumb: Satan

At first glance the selection of Satan as the dumbest of the dumb personalities of the Bible may appear strange. When we observe the work of the evil one in the Scriptures, as well as in our own lives and history, Satan appears to be anything but dumb. After all, Satan has done a lot. Shortly after the creation of the first man and woman, he brought sin and death into the world. The jealousy that prompted Cain to kill his brother Abel was his work. After God purified the world by a flood, Satan sent the pride that caused the confusion among the descendants of Noah at the tower of Babel. Satan put the lies in the mouths of Abraham and his son Isaac, as well as the meanness within Sarah's heart and the duplicity within Rebekah's spirit. He prompted Jacob's greed and Esau's shortsightedness.

Satan initiated the resentment among Jacob's sons that led them to sell their brother Joseph into Egyptian slavery. Then Satan planted lust within the heart of Potiphar's wife, which caused Joseph to be imprisoned. Satan placed a grievous yoke of slavery upon the children of Israel and then created so much dissatisfaction among them that they wandered for forty years in the wilderness before reaching the Promised Land. He corrupted Aaron, Moses' own brother, and put a rebellious spirit in Miriam, Moses' sister, and was responsible for Moses' anger and impatience, which prevented him from entering the Promised Land.

Satan turned Samson's head toward Philistine territory and was behind Haman's plot to destroy the people of God during the time of Esther. Even David, the man after God's own heart, was not immune from Satan's treachery. Satan caused Solomon to act unwisely and deafened Rehoboam's ear to sound counsel, which ended in the fracturing of the nation of Israel. Everything that Ahab and Jezebel tried to do to Israel's religious life was done through Satan's initiative. He so infiltrated the political lives of Israel and Judah that, but for a small saving and righteous remnant, they almost lost their distinctiveness as God's people.

When God's own Son came into the world, Satan fashioned the cross on which he was hung. He conspired with Judas to betray his Master and with Ananias and Sapphira to lie to the Holy Spirit. He prompted the persecution, suffering, and slaughter of the early Christians. He was behind the stoning of Stephen, the beheading of James, the crucifixion of Peter, and the banishment of John to the Isle of Patmos. To take the joy out of the revelations Paul received when he was caught up into the third heavens, Satan sent him a thorn in his flesh. And, in the book of Revelation, we see Satan establishing his throne in the city of Pergamum, the site of one of the early churches.

In our day Satan is no less busy. All of the great "isms"— racism, sexism, classism, militarism, anti-Semitism, Nazism, Fascism, atheistic communism, materialism, and conscienceless capitalism—all are his handiwork. The addictions, phobias, fears, poverty, violence, and crimes that oppress the human spirit represents his work. Yes, when one looks at all that Satan has done, he appears to be anything but dumb.

When one looks at Satan's ability to work with and work on the human spirit, he appears to be pretty smart. Satan knows just what to say and what to do to receive a hearing from the human heart. It is said that once when Satan was traveling across the desert, he met a group of friends who were trying to tempt a holy man who was devoted to a life of abstinence and meditation. They were trying to upset his spiritual equilibrium and inner peace. They tried seductions of the flesh, material possessions, hardships and trials, sickness, doubt, fear, and pain. But the holy man remained unmoved, with a peaceful expression upon his face. The devil, after watching their repeated failures, stepped forward and told his friends, "Your methods are too crude. Permit me a moment." He walked up to the holy man and said, "Have you heard the good news? While you are out here in the desert sacrificing and doing without, your brother has been selected as pastor of the biggest, finest, most prestigious, and richest church in town. Everybody is singing his praises." And as the dark scowl of jealousy and resentment came across the holy man's face, Satan walked away laughing—another victory.

When one looks at the way Satan works, he appears to be anything but dumb. He knows what strings to pull, what buttons to push, and what imperfections to play upon to get the reaction that he wants. He knows where the blind spots in our characters are, as well as where the unhealed wounds in our spirits are. He knows not only where they are but also how to reach them. More often than not he comes to us indirectly. He is aware that we would run from that which we would recognize as certain death and destruction. Therefore, the prince of darkness comes to us as an angel of light. He comes not as evil, but as good; not as an enemy, but as a friend; not as conviction, but as convenience; not as judge, but as advocate. He does not call what he offers sin, but refers to it as pleasure, fun, a good high, a good time, an easy way, and a chance to be accepted by the "in-crowd." He writes no commandments and requires no commitments.

Satan doesn't mind our coming to church or singing in the choir or serving on the board, particularly when he is still getting more of our time, energy, and money. He is happy to share with the Lord because some of his best workers are found and some of his most effective work is done in the church. We don't have to walk down an aisle to join him or manifest any newness of life to serve him. We don't have to change anything; we can stay just as we are—live the same old way, talk the same old trash, do the same old things, think the same old thoughts, drink and smoke the same old stuff, and go to the same old places. We don't have to do anything at all—just stay as we are.

Satan's work is immeasurably helped by those who do nothing, see nothing, desire to know nothing, want nothing, and hear nothing that might shake up their own little world, which amounts to nothing. Satan doesn't ask that we love him with all of our hearts, souls, and minds and love our neighbors as ourselves. Satan is satisfied with our loving only ourselves. Some of Satan's best work is carried on by those who only love themselves—their careers, their security, their comfort, their family, their race, and their friends. Thus, they don't care whom they have to hurt or use as long as they themselves are satisfied.

Since Satan comes to us as a friend, he is basically a deceiver and a liar. Thus, we can't believe anything he says, for dishonesty is his nature. Jesus said of him: "He was a murderer from the beginning, and has nothing to do with the truth, because there is no truth in him. When he lies, he speaks according to his own nature, for he is a liar and the father of lies" (John 8:44). We must closely examine everything he does. That's why the writer of Ephesians talked about resisting the "wiles of the devil" (Ephesians 6:10). Names to which he is referred in Scripture let us know that he can't be trusted. Note what the Bible calls him—Beelzebub, serpent, dragon, raging lion, evil one, accuser, tempter, destroyer, the adversary, enemy, slanderer, prince of demons, ruler of this world, prince of the power of the air, and god of this world.

The story is told of a man walking down a country road one cold winter's day. Spotting a snake that was half frozen to death, the man had compassion on it, picked it up, and put it on the inside of his coat that he might warm it and revive it. Later when the snake was revived, he bit the man.

The kind stranger dropped the snake and asked it, "How could you be so cruel as to bite me? When you were suffering and half dead, I picked you up and carried you in my bosom and revived you. Yet as soon as you are better, you bite me."

The snake looked up and said, "Remember, Mister, I'm a snake, and it's my nature to bite." Let us remember that Satan is a snake and is not to be played with or touched. If we get too close to him, he will bite. If he is picked up and carried, he will bite us every time. Judas carried him close to his bosom and ended up hanging himself. Those whose lives are being ruined by drugs, nicotine, and alcohol are persons suffering from plain old satanic snakebite.

Satan admittedly has done much, and when it comes to a knowledge of human nature, he's wise. Yet, he is still the dumbest of the dumb in the Bible. Esau may have sold his birthright for a bowl of soup; Haman may have built a gallows from which he himself was hung; Samson may have fallen to the charms of Delilah; Ananias and Sapphira may have unwittingly lied to the Holy Spirit, but Satan has consistently and intentionally challenged the Word and sovereignty of God. It's dumb to mock God and challenge God's power over life and history. Pharaoh did it and saw his armies buried in the watery grave of the Red Sea. Nebuchadnezzar did it and ended up losing his mind and eating grass like the ox. Belshazzar did it and saw a hand from out of nowhere write his doom upon the wall. Jezebel did it and was thrown over her balcony into the street, where the dogs licked her blood. Herod did it and was stricken upon his throne, and the worms ate his body.

If these servants of Satan's purposes received such a fate, then neither will their master escape the judgment of God. The book of Revelation tells me that in the end Satan will be cast into the bottomless pit into which he has cast so many who have drawn him close to their bosom. Satan's kingdom is doomed because God's Word says so, and unlike Satan, God does not lie.

Satan is dumb because he has attacked God's creation. It's dumb to believe that God, who made the creation, who gave Jesus to die for it, and the Holy Spirit to sustain it, will give it up and hand it over to Satan. Never forget that the hand who made the creation is able to maintain and protect it in spite of Satan's work. Sin may run amuck in the world, but God was able to save Noah and his family in the ark from falling rain, as well as Lot and his family in Sodom and Gomorrah from falling fire. Joseph's brothers may have sold him into slavery, and Potiphar's wife may have been responsible for his imprisonment, but God was able to use their treachery for Joseph's good and elevate him to the position of prime minister of Egypt.

It is true that Moses' error left him on the summit of Mount Nebo without entering the Promised Land, and Elijah's fear caused him to flee from Jezebel's wrath, but God was able to transport them through the corridors of time and bring them centuries later to the lonely slopes of Mount Tabor, the Mount of Transfiguration, where they personally spoke with Jesus Christ, the fulfillment of the law and the prophets. Satan may have fashioned the cross for God's only Son, but early that third day God sent an angel to roll back the stone from the tomb and raise the Son to stoop no more. In spite of Satan's destructive work, God is able to take care of the creation.

Satan may appear to be smart, but he has been outsmarted. In the early part of the last century an artist who was also a great chess player painted a picture of a chess game in which the two players were a young man and Satan. Should the young man win, he would be free from the power of evil forever. If Satan should win, the young man was to be his slave forever. The artist evidently believed in the supreme power of evil, for his picture presented the devil as the victor. The devil had made a move that left no hope for the young man. In the picture the young man's hand hovers over one of the pieces, not knowing what to do. There was no hope—the devil would win; the young man would be his slave forever. For years this picture hung in a great art gallery, and chess players from all over the world viewed the picture and reached the same conclusion—the devil wins. One day a chess player who studied the picture became convinced that there had to be a way out, and he knew of one chess player who could find it. He arranged for the supreme master of chess, an undefeated champion, to view the picture. The old man stood before the picture for more than half an hour, pondering what move the young man might make. Finally his hand paused; his eyes burned with a vision of a new combination. Suddenly he shouted, "Young man, that's the move. Make that move." To everyone's surprise, the supreme chess champion had discoverd a move that the creating artist had not considered. The conclusion was changed, the devil had been outsmarted, and the young man was forever free.

For centuries Satan held our souls in checkmate of death. Neither Abraham with his faith, Moses with the law, Job with his patience, Deborah with her courage, Esther with her obedience, David with his military skills, Solomon with his wisdom, Daniel with his vision, nor Ezekiel with his preaching could break it. But one day some two thousand years ago, God made a move that Satan hadn't counted on. God sent Jesus Christ into the world. One Friday when he bore a cross up Calvary's hill, God proclaimed, "That's the move. Make that move." The devil has been outsmarted. Because of that move, we are free forever.

7

God Has a Plan: Joseph

Text: Genesis 45:1–8

As we children of God attempt to find our way through this maze of experiences known as life, sometimes becoming lost and confused, one thing we must never forget is that God has a plan. Sometimes personal misfortune and tragedy overtake us, and circumstantial ill winds buffet us. When we have reversals in our careers, when sickness and disease attack our bodies, or when the death angel snatches a loved one from us, our faith is sometimes shaken, and we wonder why these things happen. However, in all that this maze has to offer, let us never forget that God has a plan. Sometimes we earnestly and sincerely pray, and it seems as if our prayers have fallen on deaf ears. Our requests are either denied or the answer is delayed, and we feel frustrated and forsaken. As we experience what can be the frustrations as well as the fruits of earnest prayer, we need to remember that God, whose pleasure it is to give the kingdom to God's children, does not frustrate us unless there is a reason. Therefore, when requests are denied and answers are delayed, let us remember that God has a plan.

In life, it seems, we often see the wicked prosper and scoundrels enjoy peace. The matter of theodicy or the question of suffering, particularly the suffering of the righteous coupled with the good fortune of the wicked, continues to be a very troubling and central issue for a faith that affirms the holiness and justice of an all-powerful God. Why does God allow bad things to happen to good people? How long will wrong oppress right? How much more must the good suffer by the design and at the hand of evil? When is God going to move on behalf of the innocent, the oppressed, the victimized, and the meek—those whom God's Word has said will inherit the earth? As we face what we consider to be the great injustices and contradictions of life, let us never forget that there is a divine timetable and a divine way of righting wrongs. Therefore, no matter what happens around us, no matter what we see, hear, read, or experience, let us remember that God has a plan. If anyone has questions or doubts whether God has a plan, I invite you to consider with me the story of Joseph.

Once upon a time in the land of Canaan there lived a man by the name of Jacob who had twelve sons. Among the twelve sons there was one named Joseph whom he loved more than all the others. Joseph was the child of Jacob's old age and was the first son given to him by his wife Rachel, whom he loved more than Leah or any of their handmaidens who had also borne children for him. As a token of this affection, Jacob gave to Joseph a multicolored cloak. This caused Joseph's brothers to resent him and be jealous. Now, Jacob was not denying his other sons anything in order to do something special for Joseph, for each of his sons had sufficient food, clothing, and shelter for his needs. Neither was Joseph a threat to their places in Jacob's heart or the legacy he would leave. There was sufficient livestock, land, and money to go around; and each son, by order of birth, had legal rights to his father's possessions. Yet the brothers resented the father's affection and gifts to Joseph.

We can have our share of blessings and still be jealous of the blessings that God gives to another child of God. We can have our place in the kingdom and still be jealous of what we see being done for others. We can be blessed with talent sufficient for the jobs that we've been called to do and still be jealous when another seems to be multitalented or multi-faceted. We can know and testify to God's goodness and care for us and still be jealous and resentful when God seems to bless someone else with a little more or in a different way than God blesses us.

To make matters worse, Joseph had a habit of dreaming these strange dreams and then telling the others about them. He had a dream in which he and his brothers were binding sheaves in the field, and his sheaf stood upright while the others bowed down to it. He also had another dream in which he saw the sun, the moon, and the stars bowing down to him. When Joseph told his brothers about his dreams, their resentment increased. One must be careful in sharing one's visions and dreams with others. Young people, if you want to be something in life, if you want to go places and do things, you must be careful about those with whom you share visions and dreams. People who don't see visions or have dreams, persons whose main concern is protecting their turf and doing the same old things in the same old way, will not only not understand your dream but will resent you for what they believe is the arrogance, impetuousness, and fool-ishness of your dreams.

Jealousy and resentment are terrible diseases because they can cause us to think, say, and do some terrible things. One day when his brothers were in the fields of Dothan watching over their flocks, Joseph went to them. When his brothers saw him coming from a long way off, resentment began to build in their hearts. They said, "Here comes this dreamer. Come now, let us kill him and throw him into one of the pits; then we shall say that a wild beast has devoured him, and we shall see what will become of his dreams" (Genesis 37:19–20).

Reuben, however, objected to such a foul idea, so they decided not to kill Joseph themselves, but to throw him into one of the pits. Their plans changed again when they saw an Ishmaelite caravan and decided to sell Joseph into slav-ery. They spread animal blood on his cloak and took it to

Jacob as evidence that a wild beast had killed his beloved son. They sold their brother into slavery and lied to their father. I've never seen or heard of wrong being done without a lie being required to cover up that wrong. When Joseph's brothers sold him, they assumed that they had forever ridded themselves of his presence. However, they didn't know that God had a plan for Joseph's life, and in their act of treachery and deceit, God was laying the foundation for its fulfillment.

Joseph, the object of his father's love and the victim of his brothers' resentment . . . Joseph, whose only crime was being a dreamer in the midst of nondreaming brethren . . . was taken to Egypt and there sold again, this time to Potiphar, a captain in the Egyptian army. But in accordance with God's plan, Joseph's servitude was blessed. American black people are proof positive that God will provide even in slavery. We are living witnesses that God can open doors and make ways out of no way, even in slavery.

Joseph soon became manager of Potiphar's household. But Satan will allow God's children only so much peace before he tries to disrupt their lives. One day Potiphar's wife approached Joseph with the desire to know him intimately. When Joseph spurned her advances and Potiphar's wife was convinced that he would not acquiesce to her wishes, she told her husband that it was Joseph who had made the advances toward her and that it was she who had rejected him. Potiphar then threw Joseph into prison. Thus, a second time Joseph found himself an innocent victim. The first time, his brothers' jealousy and resentment had caused him to be sold into slavery; the second time, a woman's lust and resentment had placed him in prison. When Joseph was imprisoned, Potiphar's wife assumed that she had gotten even. She didn't know, however, that God had a plan for Joseph's life and that God was using her treachery and deceit to bring it to pass.

I can just imagine that there were times during his journey from slavery to prison when Joseph must have asked "why?" and "for what?" Perhaps Joseph didn't know that God had a plan for his life and that all things were working together for his good. Every setback he encountered, every pit that was dug, every trap that was laid, and every lie that was told was leading him to where God wanted him to be. While in prison, Joseph displayed the same leadership qualities he had displayed in Potiphar's house, and soon he became the head trustee. People can't keep one of God's children down, try as they might. God's children will find a way to shine wherever they are.

While imprisoned, Joseph met the chief butler and chief baker of Pharaoh's household. They had been locked up because they had done something to anger Pharaoh. One night they both had dreams that they didn't understand. Joseph, having had experience with dreams from his childhood, was able to interpret their dreams. If God gives us a gift or a talent, God will also open up a way for that talent to be used. Joseph's interpretation spelled restoration for the butler and death for the baker. However, when the butler was restored to his position in concurrence with Joseph's interpretation, he forgot to tell Pharaoh about Joseph's case. People will forget about us once they have arrived, once they have made use of what we have to give, once they have what they need for the moment. People will forget—but where people forget, God remembers. If we forget how we have made it, God has a way of making us remember.

One night about two years later, Pharaoh had a dream that he didn't understand. He dreamed that seven fat cows were grazing by the Nile River when seven thin cows came up out of the river and devoured them. The thin cows, after eating the fat cows, were just as thin as they were before. Then he saw seven plump ears of grain growing on the same stalk. But another seven ears of blighted grain sprang up and consumed the seven plump ears. When the chief butler heard about Pharaoh's dream, he then remembered Joseph, the imprisoned Hebrew, who was a dreamer himself and seemed to have a special gift for discernment of dreams.

When the butler told Pharaoh about Joseph, the king sent for him, and Joseph interpreted the dream. He said, "The seven fat cows and the seven plump ears stand for seven years of abundant harvest in the land. But these years of plenty will be followed by seven years of famine, symbolized by the seven lean cows and the seven blighted ears. The time of famine will wipe out the seven years of abundance. What is needed is someone to oversee the harvest so that grain can be set aside in the years of abundance for the time of famine."

Pharaoh said: "I perceive you to be a wise and judicious person of integrity. I'm going to put you in charge of Operation Grain Save, and as such you will have full authority, second in command in the whole land only to me." Joseph did as he was commanded, and the seven years of abundance were followed by the years of famine, just as he said they would come to pass.

Sometime during the second year of famine over in Canaan, an old man by the name of Jacob, who had eleven sons at home, went to the grain barrel one day and saw that the supply was running low, for the famine was widespread. He told his sons, "Take money and go to Egypt, for I hear there is grain there." And as the old preachers used to say, "I can see Joseph in my mind's eye," as he stood before the storehouse that day, overseeing the sale and distribution of grain, when he saw a caravan approaching him with some familiar faces. I imagine that Joseph could hardly believe his eyes. However, before Joseph had the opportunity to react, his brothers, not recognizing him, had bowed at his feet. As they bowed, Joseph remembered his dream of the eleven sheaves and eleven stars bowing before him. If one is a child of God, one needn't worry about vengeance. For if we just follow God's plan, if we only trust and obey, at a time and in a place where it's least expected, God will bring those who try to destroy us, those who laugh at us, those who mock us, those who persecute us to our very feet.

After he had questioned them and sent them back home,

they returned, bringing their youngest brother, Benjamin, back to Egypt. Joseph invited them all to lunch, and after they had dined sufficiently, Joseph stood up and said, "Take a good look at me and tell me if you've ever seen me before." I imagine that Reuben started to raise his hand but quickly lowered it, saying, "You resemble . . . you remind me of . . . but no, no, it just can't be." I can see Joseph, when he could control his emotions no longer, break down in tears and tell them, "I am your brother Joseph, whom you plotted against and wanted to kill. I am the same Joseph whom you resented as a child; I am the same Joseph whom you mocked for his dreams. I am the same Joseph whom you lied to our father about, and I am the same Joseph you lowered into the pit and sold into slavery. But do not grieve, for I bear you no ill will. You must answer to the God who preserved me in spite of that which you tried to do to me. For you see, God had a plan for my life. God allowed you to lower me into a pit and sell me into slavery many years ago that I might feed you at my table at this very moment. So it was not you who sent me here, but God—who watched over me and preserved me by power divine and made me a ruler in the land of Egypt."

I'm so glad that God has a plan for our lives. When we finish playing games with one another and on one another, when we finish our politics and schemes, our tricks and designs, I'm so glad that God has a plan for each and every one of us. And what always fascinates me about God's plan is that God is able to take the evil that people design for our undoing and downfall and turn it around so that it works for our good. Joseph later said to his brothers, "You meant evil against me, but God meant it for good."

I'm so glad that God has a plan for our lives. For Jesus came in accordance with God's plan. When Satan decided that he would hold humanity captive, God had a plan for our redemption. Wrapped in love, grace, and truth, God stepped across time and was born as a baby in Bethlehem. He grew into a man who refused to compromise with wrong, and when Satan and the forces of evil decided that they would destroy him by subjecting him to the worst possible death they knew—death on the cross—Jesus declared that he would take that same cross that degraded others and use it as the pledge for our redemption. For he said: "And I, if I be lifted up from the earth, will draw all men unto me" (John 12:32, KJV). The cross that evil used to shame a perfect Christ became God's plan and a pledge for our redemption.

> Tempted and tried we're oft made to wonder
> Why it should be thus all the day long,
> While there are others living about us,
> Never molested, though in the wrong.
>
> Farther along we'll know all about it,
> Farther along we'll understand why;
> Cheer up, my brother, live in the sunshine,
> We'll understand it all by and by.[1]

[1]"Farther Along," words by W. B. Stevens, Copyright © 1937 by Stamps Baxter Music/BMI. All rights reserved. Used by permission of The Benson Co., Inc., Nashville, TN.

8

Little People in Big Places: Abimelech

Text: Judges 9:7–15

The longer I live and the more I see, the more I am made aware of the fact that big places are often occupied by little people. We meet them on our jobs, in our schools, in our families, in our communities, fraternal organizations, social clubs, lodges, and churches. Sometimes we see them in government, where they can affect the lives of hundreds, thousands, or even millions of people in a town, state, or a nation—little people in big places. Sometimes they have three or four degrees, and sometimes they have none; sometimes they are professionals—doctors, lawyers, preachers, teachers—and sometimes they're not. Sometimes they are young, and sometimes they are old; sometimes they have plenty of money, and sometimes they don't; sometimes they are black, and sometimes they are white; sometimes they are men, and sometimes they are women.

Somehow these persons have managed to be in positions that have some authority or clout, ones that require us to show some respect. Yet in spite of the size of the office, the power of the position, or the weight of the responsibility, they remain little people. In terms of their thinking and ideas, their vision and attitudes towards others, the way they use their offices, positions, or power, they are still very small people in big places. They don't make the office; the office makes them. They don't run the position; the position runs them. They don't have the power; the power has them. They are little people in big places.

The story that surrounds our text is about a little person who managed to land in a big place. When Gideon, the famous judge and military general of Israel who defeated the huge Midianite army with only three hundred soldiers, passed away, he was an old man with seventy-one sons. Seventy were by his many wives, and the other by one of his concubines. It was Abimelech, the concubine's son, who decided that he ought to be the king. So, soon after Gideon's death he went to the elders of the town of Shechem, which was one of the major cities of the land, and persuaded them to support him in his campaign to be king. He told them, "You know Gideon had seventy legitimate sons and each one wants to be king, and each has a legitimate claim to the throne. Therefore, the kingdom stands to be divided seventy ways. Now do you want to be ruled by seventy kings, or would you prefer being ruled by one—namely me?"

Let us note briefly that Abimelech had no right to say that all seventy of Gideon's sons wanted to be king. Abimelech just assumed that all of them wanted to be king just because he wanted to be king. People often think that everyone is like them and that everybody wants what they want. There are some pastors who believe that every other preacher is after their church. There are officers who believe that every new member of the club is after their office. There are presidents who believe every club member wants to be president. There are supervisors on jobs who believe that every other employee wants their job. There are persons who believe that everybody is dishonest and a liar because they themselves are that way. There are still others who believe that because they are sincere, everybody else is also. However, if we are going to have a realistic approach to people and life, the first thing we must remember is that for good or bad, everybody is not like us. Everybody doesn't have our virtues or our faults.

The elders of Shechem decided that since Abimelech's mother came from their town and therefore Abimelech was closer to being one of them than any of the others, they would support him in his aspirations. They chose to support Abimelech, not because he was most qualified or a good candidate, but because he was one of them! They figured he might be more kindly disposed toward them and their interests. Very few people think in terms of what's best for everybody. Most of us are only concerned about "What's in it for me?" We will go along with a lesser candidate if we believe that we can have some influence or run the person who is elected or appointed over us.

When Abimelech received the support of the elders of Shechem, he hired what the Living Bible calls some "worthless loafers who agreed to do whatever he told them to." Little people surround themselves with other little people. If you really want to know what a person is like, look at the people that he or she chooses as friends and intimates. If a person is petty, gossipy, or set in his or her ways, the people with whom he or she associates will be the same way. But if a person has character, intelligence, vision, refinement, and religion, those who are chosen for friends and associates are usually like-minded.

Abimelech, with his big ambition and narrow vision, conspired with his cohorts of equally small vision to execute the other seventy sons of Gideon. Abimelech coveted the highest office in the land, yet he was willing to use the lowest methods to obtain it. He was prepared to kill to get what he wanted. It's bad to want something so desperately that one doesn't care who one hurts or what one does to get it. We can identify a little person not simply by the size of his or her ambition, but by what he or she is willing to do to get there. No matter how noteworthy the venture or how noble the goal, when getting there becomes more important than how one gets there or more important than the kind of person one must become to get there, then that person may be in a big place but still be a little person. For people tend to remain what they were before they reached their goals. If a person was a liar or scoundrel before, he or she will be the same thing after. If a preacher did little as a pastor, he or she will not do much as a bishop or moderator. If a person did nothing as a member, don't expect much from that person as an officer. If a coworker was a stooge and flunky as our peer, don't expect much else from him or her as a supervisor. If a politician was a crook before he was elected, don't expect him or her to reform once elected.

When we have little or no qualms about what we do to get what we want, we do two things. First, we reduce what we are after. Martin Luther King, Jr., was right—there is an intrinsic, inextricable relationship between the means and the end. Moral ends cannot be achieved and cannot be justified by immoral means. We can no more defend truth with a lie, or support right by doing wrong, than we can come back from where we've never been. Second, we reduce ourselves. "For what does it profit a man, to gain the whole world and forfeit his life? For what can a man give in return for his life?" (Mark 8:36–37).

Abimelech almost succeeded in killing all of Gideon's seventy sons; but the youngest, Jotham, escaped. The Abimelechs of history may kill off most of the sons, but the Lord is always going to allow one to escape. Pharaoh may kill off the Hebrew males, but the Lord is going to save a Moses. Jezebel may kill off the prophets, but the Lord is going to save an Elijah. Ahab may buy off the prophets, but the Lord is going to save a Micaiah. Herod may kill off the young males under two years of age, but the Lord is going to save a Jesus. White society may emasculate thousands of black males, but the Lord is going to save a Richard Allen, a Frederick Douglas, a Martin Luther King, Jr., or a Malcolm X. That same society may suppress the black female, but the Lord will save a Sojourner Truth, a Harriet Tubman, a Mary McLeod Bethune, a Mahalia Jackson, or a Barbara Jordan.

When Jotham, the son who escaped, heard about Abimelech's coronation, he stood upon Mount Gerizim and shouted to the men of Shechem the parable that serves as our text. He said:

"The trees once went forth to anoint a king over them, and they said to the olive tree, 'Reign over us.' But the olive tree said to them, 'Shall I leave my fatness, by which gods and men are honored and come to sway over the trees?' Then the trees said to the fig tree, 'Come you, and reign over us.' But the fig tree said to them, 'Shall I leave my sweetness and my good fruit, and go to sway over the trees?' And the trees said to the vine, 'Come you, and reign over us.' But the vine said to them, 'Shall I leave my wine which cheers the gods and men, and go to sway over the trees?' Then all the trees said to the bramble, 'Come you, and reign over us.' And the bramble said, 'If in good faith you are anointing me king over you, then come and take refuge in my shade; but if not, let fire come out of the bramble and devour the cedars of Lebanon'"(Judges 9:8–15).

The first act of the thorn bush was to change the nature of the kingship from one of serving to one of being served. Little people in big places always use their office to serve themselves and make themselves look big, and not to serve others. Little people in big places always use their positions of power and prestige to exploit and oppress those who put them where they are. Little people in big places cannot exercise the command of Jesus, who said: "You know that the rulers of the Gentiles lord it over them, and their great men exercise authority over them. It shall not be so among you; but whoever would be great among you must be your servant" (Matthew 20:25–26).

"Well," somebody might ask, "Tell me, preacher, how do little people get into big places?" That's easy, remember the men of Shechem supported Abimelech, and the trees asked the thorn bush. The only way evil can stand is when it is supported by good. The illegal numbers racket and the black market would not be as lucrative as they are without the support of good, decent, faithful church folk. Tyrants are placed and maintained by good people. The government could not exploit the colored people of the Third World without the backing of the American Christian Church. Businesses would not be able to stay open on Sundays if

Christian didn't shop in them and if Christian workers refused to work in them on Sundays. Gossip and lies would
not circulate around the church if Christians didn't listen to
them and repeat them.

Also remember, the thorn bush was asked to be king only
because all the others turned down this offer. Whenever
good and decent people refuse to become involved in the
church and the community, the way is opened for little
people to get into big places. Whenever sincere, intelligent
people who have the best interests of the church at heart
refuse to become involved because they are either too busy
or don't feel like being bothered, the way is opened for little
people to get into big places. Whenever good people get
tired and disgusted and quit, the way is opened for little
people to get into big places. Whenever good people are so
tired or busy that they can't find time to learn what's happening in our children's schools and get involved in the local
Parent-Teacher Association (P.T.A.), the way is left open for
little people to get into big places. Whenever we don't vote,
we leave the way open for little people to get into big places.
Whenever we don't keep abreast of what's happening in our
community and let the others run the communities in which
we live, work, and pay taxes, we leave the way open for little
people to get into big places. Whenever we say, "Let somebody else do it," or "It makes no difference to me," or "I
don't have time to be bothered," we leave the way open for
little people to get into big places.

The only defense we have against the thorns is our own
involvement and participation. An experience in the life of
the prophet Isaiah can serve as a paradigm for us. One day
in the year that King Uzziah died, Isaiah went to the temple.
While there he saw the Lord, high and lifted up, with his
train filling the temple. Above the throne stood the seraphims, each of whom had six wings. With two wings they
covered their face, with two wings they covered their feet,
and with two wings they flew. As they flew they cried,
"Holy, holy, holy is the LORD of hosts; the whole earth is full
of his glory." The posts of the door were moved and the

whole house was filled with smoke. Then Isaiah cried: "Woe is me! for I am lost; for I am a man of unclean lips, and I dwell in the midst of a people of unclean lips; for my eyes have seen the King, the LORD of hosts!"(Isaiah 6:5). Then one of the seraphims flew to Isaiah with a live coal that had been taken with the tongs from off the altar. He laid it upon Isaiah's mouth and said: "Behold, this has touched your lips, your guilt is taken away, and your sin forgiven." Then Isaiah also heard the voice of the Lord saying, "Whom shall I send, and who will go for us?" Then Isaiah said, "Here am I! Send me" (Isaiah 6: 7–8). It wasn't enough for Isaiah to rejoice in the experience of his own salvation and redemption. When the question was asked, "Whom shall I send, and who will go for us?" Isaiah had to respond: "Here am I! Send me."

It would also have been easy for Jesus Christ to decline the opportunity to become involved with sinful humanity. He could have said, "Shall I leave heaven with all of its glory, the angels and archangels, the seraphim and cherubim, the glory and beauty of heaven, to go to earth and live among men?" Instead, he took the challenge of redeeming sinful women and men. And, because he came, sinful persons though we are, we have become heirs of an inheritance undefiled, incorruptible, reserved in heaven for us. Jesus had to answer the call for humankind's redemption. In his own way he had to say, "Here am I! Send me." The church will only be what it ought to be; our communities and schools will only be what they should be when good, decent people become involved and say, "Here we are! Send us." Liberation will come only when you and I are moved to lift our vision and level of concern beyond our personal agenda so that we don't allow the little people to take over. We must be prepared to say, "Here am I! Send me."

When I was a little boy, people used to sing:

> I'll go, I'll go;
> I'll go, I'll go;
> If the Lord wants somebody,
> Here am I, send me, send me.

9

He Had It but He Lost It: Saul

Text: 1 Samuel 15:22–23

Among the many personalities whom we meet in the Scriptures, Saul, the son of Kish, has to be one of the most tragic. He was a man who had everything going for him and lost it all. To begin with, he came from a good family. His father was a rich and influential individual who belonged to the tribe of Benjamin. Further, Saul was a person with a striking appearance. The Scriptures describe him as the most handsome man in the kingdom, a man whose stature was of such that he stood head and shoulders above everyone else. He was a responsible young man. When some of the family's livestock escaped, Saul was the one sent to look for them. He had a humble spirit. When the prophet Samuel informed him that all of Israel would, in a sense, be his possession, Saul protested that he was from one of the smallest tribes and that Samuel must have picked the wrong man. He had charismatic leadership gifts. In times of crisis he knew how to step in and take charge of the situation, and people responded to his clarion call. Most importantly, Saul was the individual whom the Lord had chosen to be Israel's king. Out of all the young, erudite, and pious men, Saul was the one that the Spirit instructed Samuel to anoint as Israel's first king.

Saul undoubtedly had more initial support, and enthusiasm was probably higher at the outset of his reign than for any subsequent king in Israel's history. After all, Saul was Israel's first king, and there is always something special about our first.

The first has special place in our hearts. Parents remember a child's first word, and they anticipate that child making its first steps. Whether it's our first child, our first love, our first job, our first date, the first time we met someone special, our first pair of heels, our first car, our first home, or the first time we felt the Spirit of the Lord, we never forget our first. Because it is the first, there is always a sense of hope and expectation and perhaps naiveté—feelings that life and experience manage to temper somewhat by the time we reach the second or the third. Because he was the first, Saul had the opportunity to set the standard for Israel's monarchs for generations to come. There were no precedents to follow. Saul didn't have to listen to citizens tell him that "when King So and So was here, we did it like this . . . ." Saul had freedom, and because he was the first and the Israelites had had no experience in dealing with their own king, they were willing to do whatever was necessary to please him. They were willing to trust him totally and follow him without reservation.

The record shows that Saul started off doing a good job. He began to meld the loose confederation of Israelite tribes into a unified kingdom. Although the kingdom expanded greatly under David and reached its zenith under Solomon, the foundation for its growth and development was laid by Saul. He drove the Philistines out of much of the interior of the land of Israel and pushed them back to the frontiers. The more success the Lord allowed him to achieve, the more powerful he became. Success and power however are not self-perpetuating. Reaching the top is no guarantee that we will automatically stay there. Becoming an initial success is one thing; knowing how to handle success so that one can stay on top and be a continued success is quite another. Attaining power is one thing; knowing how to use power once it has been attained is quite another. While we are striving for success and seeking power, we had better make sure that we know how to use them once we have made whatever sacrifices that were necessary to attain them. Not everyone can handle success and power. There are people who are failures, not because they didn't reach the top, but because they didn't know what to do with success and power once they reached the top. Success and power can break us as quickly as they can make us. It has been said, "Those whom the gods would destroy they first make mad with power."

Success and power are deceiving as well as seductive. They can cause us to think more highly of ourselves than we should. With their pleasant music in our ears and their sweet smell in our nostrils, it's easy for us to start believing that whatever we've done, we've done by ourselves, that we cannot be moved, and that we are accountable to no one but ourselves. However, everyone is accountable to someone or something. People do not have the right to do whatever they want, however they want, whenever they want, to whomever they want with impunity—without having to answer for it at some point to someone or something. When I was a boy, I used to say, "I'll be glad when I grow up and can do just as I please." However, it wasn't long after becoming a man that I discovered that there always has been and there always will be some force, person, or circumstance in my life to hold me in check. That force may be persons such as parents, spouse, children, or other family members. That force may be friends, associates, or others who "knew us when" and don't mind telling us that we are "beside ourselves." Our employers, our jobs, our responsibilities and obligations may cause us to pause and consider before we speak or act. That force may be conscience or our faith or the home training that reminds us that we should know better than to do the things we do or act the way we act. But all of us have some regulating force in our lives that holds the reigns on our foolishness, that prevents us from turning

God-given freedom and opportunities into irresponsible license.

Saul had such a force in his life, and his name was Samuel, the prophet. If no one else knew, Samuel knew; if Saul himself had forgotten, Samuel had not forgotten the nature of Saul's kingship. When success and power began to go to Saul's head, Samuel was there to remind him that he did not come to the throne by his own hand. He did not orchestrate any military coup to get to the throne. He had not been voted into office. He wasn't the only available person for the throne. He might not even have been Samuel's personal choice. Saul was king for one reason and one reason only— the Lord, God, Yahweh, the stacker of mountains and the scooper of valleys, the pathfinder through the Red Sea and the shaker of Jericho's walls, had declared that, "This is the man that I want to be king." Thus, Saul was called, not to be Israel's king, but to be God's king over Israel. He was not to rule like any other king; he was to rule according to the will of God. Let us never forget that God does not call us to be common and ordinary, but we are called to be a people set apart, holy, and consecrated to doing God's will.

Saul, however, chose to rule in his way, forgetting who had put him where he was. We have to be careful about burning the bridges that brought us over. Saul forgot that whatever the Lord gives, the Lord can take away. We have to be careful about misusing and abusing what God has given us. If we don't use what God has given us in the right way and with the right spirit, we will lose it. God gives us health, but if we fail to take care of our bodies, we will lose our health. God gives us talents, but if we fail to use them in the way that God desires, we can lose them. God gives us opportunities, but if we fail time and time again to make the most of those opportunities, God will not continue to cast pearls, as it were, before swine. Opportunity will cease to knock on our doors. God gives us the Spirit, but if we resist the Spirit often enough and long enough, we will drive the Spirit away.

Saul thought he could disregard God's Word and will. He thought he could sin and then use sacrifices to patch things up between himself and God. God knows when we are real. God knows when we are trying to bargain with heaven. God knows whether or not we will be able to keep the vows we make. God knows when we intend to do right, even if we later do wrong. God knows when we have no intention of doing right. God knows when we are treating religion like some good luck charm that we keep with us so nothing bad will happen to us.

God knew Saul's heart, and that's why God sent Samuel to Saul one day after Saul had sinned once too often. There is such a thing as sinning once too often. David said, "The LORD is merciful and gracious, slow to anger and abounding in steadfast love. He will not always chide, nor will he keep his anger for ever" (Psalm 103: 8–9). So when Saul had sinned once too often and was making a sacrifice for his wrongdoings, Samuel confronted him and said,

> "Has the LORD as great delight in burnt offerings and
>   sacrifices,
>   as in obeying the voice of the LORD?
> Behold, to obey is better than sacrifice,
>   and to hearken than the fat of rams.
> For rebellion is as the sin of divination,
>   and stubbornness is as iniquity and idolatry.
> Because you have rejected the word of the LORD,
>   he has also rejected you from being king."
>   —1 Samuel 15:22–23

Saul was a man who had it, but he lost it.

After Saul lost his kingdom, he became a different person. Sin not only changes our circumstances externally, it changes us internally. It affects not only what we have but also what we are. It gives us another personality—one that is a distorted and disfigured version of our true self. Sin and remorse had reduced Saul to a shell of his former self. This personable, charismatic, handsome young man became an irritable, disgruntled, haunted, and driven old man who was difficult to live with. He became suspicious of everyone around him. When we become distrustful and suspicious of everyone, we have a serious problem with self. When we start believing that everyone is out to get us and everyone wants our kingdom, we have a serious problem with self. When we start believing that no one likes us and everybody is against us, we have a serious problem with self.

Saul turned on those closest to him who were trying the most to comfort and help him. He had a young armorbearer and soldier by the name of David who began to score victories on behalf of his king. At first Saul was pleased with the service David was rendering. However, when the people began to sing, "Saul has killed his thousands and David his tens of thousand," Saul's insecurity and jealousy drove him to distraction. When we are threatened by another person's successes, we have a serious problem with self. When we can't stand to see another person do well, when we lose sleep over it and pout and fret about it, we have a serious problem wilh self.

Soon Saul found himself battling the Philistines again (the enemy never stops coming). This time, however, he had a reduced army because he had driven David and a number of his more able soldiers away from him, and the battle was going against him. It's hard to fight life's battles when we have driven the Spirit away. The battle will go against us every time when we are fighting without God's presence because we are fighting with severely reduced forces. We are fighting without the power we need to attain victory. Saul was mortally wounded and asked his armorbearer to kill him, lest the Philistines capture him and torture him. When the armorbearer refused, Saul fell on his own sword and killed himself. What a tragic ending to the life of a man who had everything going for him.

Saul was a man who had it, but he lost it. He lost his kingdom, he lost his health, he lost his mind, he lost God's Spirit, he lost his friends, he lost his supporters, he lost his life. We can have everything going for us, but if we don't have the Lord in our lives, we can still lose. On the other hand, we can start off with little or nothing, but if we have the Lord in our lives and on our side, if we are anchored in God's love and are committed do doing God's will, if our hearts are fixed and our minds set on serving God, if we abide in Jesus and Jesus abides in us, then the whole world can be ours.

Let us remember another king. Unlike Saul, who had everything going for him, this king had almost everything going against him. Saul came from a rich family. This king was the earthly son of a carpenter and a humble handmaiden. Saul was a dashing, handsome, and striking figure whose appearance and stature stood out. This king was rather average looking. The prophet Isaiah said of him that "he had no form or comeliness that we should look at him, and no beauty that we should desire him" (Isaiah 53:2). During his reign, Saul possessed houses and lands. But this king said of himself: "Foxes have holes, and birds of the air have nests; but the Son of man has no where to lay his head" (Matthew 8:20). To entice his soldiers to follow him to war, Saul could promise them a share of the spoils. This king offered his followers a cross. He said, "If any man would come after me, let him deny himself and take up his cross and follow me" (Matthew 16:24).

In other words, Saul was an affluent king, but this other king went through life borrowing everything. It has been said that he was born in a borrowed stable. He preached from a borrowed boat. When he fed the multitudes, he had to borrow a little boy's lunch of two fish and five barley loaves. He rode on a borrowed mule into Jerusalem. He held his Last Supper with his disciples in a borrowed upper room. When he died, he was buried in a borrowed tomb. His only possessions were his clothes (which were divided amongst the soldiers who crucified him) and his cross. The sins that made up the cross were not his, but were borrowed from you and me. But despite all that he lacked materially, he had something that the world couldn't give you and the world can't take away. He had God, who early that third day, while it was yet dark, raised him to stoop no more and to proclaim that "Power, all power is given into my hands."

He is the King of my life. That's why when the choice is between the world's power and riches and Jesus, I say, "Give me Jesus." In the morning when I rise, "Give me Jesus." When my soul is tossed and driven and my heart is filled with pain and my thinking is totally confused, "Give me Jesus." When Satan has assaulted me and I don't have strength to fight anymore, "Give me Jesus." The reknowned pulpiteer Dr. Gardner Taylor said, "Not Moses, for he says I must be clean to come to the mercy seat. Not Socrates, for he tells me I must have knowledge to reach the Summum Bonum, the absolute good. Not Buddha, for he tells me I must give up all that is material before I may enter life. Not John the Baptist, for he tells me I must bring 'Fruits worthy of repentance.' "[1]

> I'd rather have Jesus than silver or gold,
> I'd rather be His than have riches untold;
>
> He's all that my hungering spirit needs,
> I'd rather have Jesus and let Him lead
>
> Than to be the king of a vast domain
> Or be held in sin's dread sway;
> I'd rather have Jesus than anything
> This world affords today.[2]

---

[1]Gardner C. Taylor, *The Scarlet Thread.* Elgin: Progressive Baptist Publishing House, 1981, p. 83.

[2]"I'd Rather Have Jesus," words by Rhea F. Miller, Copyright © 1922, 1950. Copyright renewed 1939, 1966 by Chancel Music, Inc. Assigned to the Rodeheaver Co. (A Division of Word, Inc.). All Rights Reserved. International Copyright Secured. Used by Permission.

10

Doing What Has to Be Done: Benaiah

Text: 1 Chronicles 11:22–23

Although all honest ways of earning a living are honorable, all honest ways of earning a living are not glamorous. All work done in a home may be necessary, but all housework may not be exciting. All schoolwork may be important; however, all schoolwork may not be interesting. All sincere and inspired church work may lead to eternal life; however, all sincere and inspired church work does not have eternal significance. Earthly life would be heavenly indeed if it was solely filled with glamorous, exciting, interesting, and eternally significant tasks. Life, however, is also filled with nonglamorous, unexciting, uninteresting, and uneventful things which must still be done if life is to be complete or even livable. A big-time politician with celebrity status is glamorous; a garbage worker is not. Yet life in this society would become a living hell of disease, decay, and discomfort without the unexciting and dirty work of the garbage man. We tend to run toward the glamorous and run away from the apparently insignificant. However, blessed is the person who is willing to do what has to be done.

Benaiah, one of David's noble warriors, was such a person. David was a great king of long tenure, not only because of his own personal courage and fighting abilities, but also because he developed noble and loyal warriors who fought by his side. These warriors fought not only with David but also for him when he could not personally be present and when he became too old to fight any longer. David's warriors, then, had not only great fighting skill but also something else that makes the difference between a winning and a losing army, a championship and a mediocre team, a family rather than a group of related people, a community of believers rather than a congregation of acquaintances. They had commitment to their cause, loyalty to their leader, and a sense of camaraderie. It doesn't take much loyalty or devotion to fight by a person's side when he or she is present. One can do so out of one's own need to survive politically. True nobility and loyalty come forth when the leaders are absent and the troops stay together and fight just as hard for the cause. That's what it means to be a true army, family, team, or community of believers—to remain loyal and committed to one another in spite of all.

Benaiah was one of David's bravest warriors. Benaiah fought two fierce soldiers of Moab, either one of whom would have been more than a match for an ordinary soldier, and emerged the victor. Then, after slaying a lion, Benaiah also slew an Egyptian giant who carried a spear like a "weaver's beam." Brave warriors face great opponents, the kind that would overwhelm the ordinary soldier.

Brave faith faces great tests, the kind that mediocre religion is unable to stand up against. Only brave faith would consider giving up its most dearly beloved on Mount Moriah in obedience to the Word of God. Only brave faith can swim against the tide of public opinion and declare that the land can be conquered and giants defeated, while others see themselves as grasshoppers and victims. Only brave faith can defy kings' edicts and remain vigilant in prayer and even refuse to bow to golden images at the risk of careers and life. Only brave faith can undertake great things for God and do great things through God.

Only a brave church can undertake great challenges. While some churches shrink from great risks, fearing failure, the brave church understands that nothing is too hard for God. The brave church remembers that the God whom they serve owns the cattle upon a thousand hills and all the world's silver and gold, and God has promised to supply all God's children's needs according to God's riches both in the earth and in glory.

Benaiah was not only loyal and brave but also conscientious. He was willing to do what had to be done. Our text recounts an incident in which a pit had been dug to trap a marauding lion. Snow had fallen and effectively hidden the trap. The lion had fallen into the trap and was vainly trying to escape. No one wanted the unpleasant task of descending into the pit to slay the lion. However, if the community was to live in peace again, someone would have to face the lion. If children were going to play in the pastures again without fear, if the women were going to be able to carry their pitchers to the community without fear, if farmers were to be able to go to and from their fields without fear, if travelers and visitors were to be able to use the roads without fear— then someone would have to slay the lion.

Benaiah had nothing to gain by doing it; he already had enough honors attached to his name. His bravery had already been established through his many exploits on the battlefield. He didn't need to fight lions to advance his career. He was already ranked as one of David's top thirty warriors and was commander of the king's bodyguard. He could have easily directed one of the soldiers under his command to discharge this unpleasant task. Conscientious people, however, don't assign others to tasks simply because they have the authority. Conscientious people do not assign tasks to others simply because those tasks are something they personally prefer not doing. If there is something that has to be done, whether there's any personal glory in it or not, whether it's unpleasant or not, whether they are asked or not—if no one else is doing it, conscientious people step forward and do what has to be done.

Satisfaction for the conscientious person doesn't come

from the praise or rewards of people. Their reward is the satisfaction they feel in knowing they were able to solve a problem, lend a helping hand, or meet a need when something had to be done. Benaiah was a conscientious person. Consequently, on that snowy day, when others were huddled inside in comfort around warm fires, he went down into the pit by himself, without a crowd of onlookers, well-wishers, or faultfinders, and did what needed to be done. He slew the lion and brought peace again to the community.

Thank God for those who do what has to be done. Thank God for those in the family who, when the other family members become insulated in their own personal concerns and isolated in their own lives, do what has to be done to hold the family together. Thank God for those in the family who don't forget about the elderly members, who take the time to guide the young, who don't forget to call and minister to the sick members of the family. Many times the tasks are time-consuming, nerve-rattling or unpleasant. However, if a family is to be a family indeed, then these unheralded tasks have to be done.

Thank God for church members who see a need and do what has to be done. Thank God for church members who say, "Reverend, you don't have to call my name. I can't do what others do, so I'm doing what I can. I don't want any pay, because God has been good to me. I'm just trying to give to the church in my own way because I love the Lord and I love the church, and I'm grateful for what the church means in my life. So whatever I can do, I'm willing to do." Some people see a need but sit back and wait to be asked. No one knows their ability or desire to work. Yet they will become angry and complain that the same people are used over and over again. Hear them as they say, "The pastor always calls on her," or "He acts as if Brother Jones is the only man in the church."

People are used again and again because they have shown in the past that they are reliable and that they can be counted on to do what has to be done. They have established a track record of faithfulness. And what about the complainers? They need to step forward to meet the needs instead of sitting back and waiting for someone to notice them or beg them to help. Then next time maybe the preacher won't have to use the same persons. He or she will know about those other capable people because in an hour of need they stepped forward and did what had to be done.

Some of the tasks are not glamorous to be sure: cleaning the church, cooking food, repairing the building, working in the office, mimeographing or folding bulletins, providing transportation for the elderly, feeding the hungry, ministering to the destitute, visiting the sick, listening to someone else's problems, maintaining the records, attending long and sometimes heated meetings, soothing hurt egos—these are not glorious works. However, if the church is to be a caring community, if it is to be administered in a sound business manner, if God's house is to be kept beautiful, then someone has to be willing to do what has to be done

Some of these nonglamorous tasks may be personally inconvenient, and perhaps some of them may be someone else's official responsibility. However, if the job isn't being done, why not offer a helping hand? Why not offer suggestions? Some of them, if not all of them, just might be accepted. Why can't we be the persons who are willing to go down into the pits of nonglamourous service? Why can't we be the persons who say the words to restore peace when confusion has arisen? Why can't our hands be the ones to drive a nail, lift a broom, or send out a letter? If the needs of the young people are not being met, why don't we try to meet them? If the sick are not receiving proper attention, why don't we volunteer? If the aged are being neglected, why don't we give them some of our time? Why can't we be those persons who are willing to stand in the gap between problems and solutions, between needs and fulfillment? Why can't we be the persons who stand ready to say:

"If the Lord wants somebody;
Here am I; send me! I'll go!"

We live a redeemed life today and have hope of life eternal because when we were in the pit of sin and were being terrorized by a lion called death, Jesus, our mighty warrior, came down into the pit one Good Friday and set us free. I once read a story about a man who dreamed that he fell into a deep dark well. He first called for help until he became hoarse, but no one heard him. He began to try to climb out, but his fingers couldn't get a decent grip on the slippery sides of the well. He would climb so far and fall back down. Finally, with his fingers bloodied, he gave up trying to climb out of the well and called again for help.

This time a passerby heard him and said, "I can't get you out of the well, but I can make it more comfortable for you." He dropped a bottle of liquor into the well, and after the man drank it, the well didn't seem so bad after all. However, after a while sobriety returned, as it always does, and the man began to be miserable again.

A woman appeared and said: "I can't get you out of the well, but things could be worse. Accept your situation and make the best of it." The man tried not to feel sorry for himself and to be grateful that he was alive, but that didn't work. He was still miserable and alone, and despair maintained its grip upon his spirit. He started to climb again; after all, he had always been able to take care of himself. But bloody, cold, and hungry, he slid back into the bottom of the well.

Then another man appeared at the top of the well and said, "I can get you out of the well, but you have to trust me." The man in the well didn't know how the man would rescue him, but he knew that he couldn't deliver himself, so he told the man, "Yes, I'll trust you." Then Jesus Christ did what none of the others had been willing or able to do. He jumped into the well himself, and upon the Master's shoulders, the man stood and climbed out of the well, and Jesus remained in his place.

Some two thousand years ago, Jesus did what had to be done.

> He was wounded for our transgressions,
>   he was bruised for our iniquities;
> upon him was the chastisement that made us whole,
>   and with his stripes we are healed."
> —Isaiah 53:5

If we have been lifted by Jesus, then the command comes to us—do what has to be done and lift someone else.

11

From the Bitter to the Sweet: Naomi

Text: Ruth 1:19–21

The words of heartache, disappointment, and anguish that constitute the text are from the lips of one of the Bible's great but gentle sufferers. When we think of those in the Scripture who suffered much, our minds automatically turn to Job and possibly to Jeremiah, the prophet who personally internalized the pain that he saw coming upon his people. When we think of those who suffered much for the cause of Christ, we naturally think of Paul, and John on Patmos, or Peter, who was crucified upside down, or the other disciples, and the many nameless martyrs who chose to die rather than deny their faith. However, among those who have suffered, Jesus still set the example as one who met his trouble with determination, endured his pain with dignity, bore his cross with grace, lived through his loneliness with faith, and faced death without fear. His agony in the Garden of Gethsemane and his crucifixion on Calvary are the two greatest scenes of suffering in Scripture.

The list of those in Scripture who suffered much would not be complete, however, without Naomi, whose life is chronicled in the Book of Ruth. This book is as much about her as it is about her daughter-in-law, after whom it was named. One day many centuries ago, the sun rose upon the land of Palestine, and daylight revealed earth that was parched and dusty and fields that were barren. Palestine at this time was in the midst of a severe famine. Every crust of bread and grain of wheat, barley, or corn became a valued commodity and was carefully monitored so that none would be wasted. As people eked out a living and struggled to survive, they considered their options and their futures. Some old-timers, who had experienced famines before, counselled those who were despairing to hold tight, sit still, wait for God until things got better. Most people decided to wait out the famine. There were those, however, who decided to move elsewhere until times got better. Among those who decided to relocate was a young man named Elimelech. Thus, with a mood of sadness and many tearful good-byes, Elimelech, his young and beautiful wife, Naomi, and their two sons traveled to the land of Moab to begin life anew.

In time the famine ended in Palestine. Elimelech, having become comfortable in Moab, decided to remain there with his family. Sorrow, however, beset the small household when Elimelech suddenly died, leaving Naomi with the challenge of rearing two sons in a foreign land. The Lord strengthened Naomi for the tasks that she faced and made ways for her. Naomi survived her loss and reared her sons, who grew up and married two Moabite girls. One son married a young lady named Orpah, and the other married a young woman named Ruth.

Naomi assumed the role of the gentle and helpful matriarch of the family and was kind to her daughters-in-law. Although she lived near them, she never interfered in their lives. Naomi maintained a comfortable closeness with a healthy distance. Hers was a closeness that did not smother and a distance that did not alienate. The key to maintaining any relationship is found in striking the right balance between closeness and distance. No one wants a love that smothers. Everyone has the need, as well as the right, to private space and independence.

Naomi's family knew that she was close if needed and ready to assist if asked. And Naomi waited to be asked.

However, if she took the initiative in offering a suggestion or a helping hand, she sought the proper time and the proper way. Sometimes our offer of help is rejected because it is offered in the wrong way. People do not want to feel beholden simply because someone else helps. They don't want their self-respect demeaned, their feelings disregarded, and their dignity trampled upon because someone is helping them. We're quick to say, "I offered my assistance, but they acted as if they didn't want it, so forget them." If someone is in need and doesn't want our help, maybe we should ask why. The problem might be their attitude, but it could be our attitude when we made the offer. Sometimes we offer help grudgingly or condescendingly. People may be in need, but they can still read our attitudes. Being helpful means more than having resources; it also means having the proper attitude and being sensitive to the feelings of others.

Evidently Naomi was able to strike the right balance between closeness and distance and was able to offer her assistance in the right way because she won the genuine love and respect, and not simply the tolerance, of her daughters-in-law. They started referring to her as "Mother," and a spirit of peace existed in their family. Things went well for about ten years, when tragedy stuck again. Within a short period of time, both of Naomi's sons died. As matriarch of the family, Naomi assumed the responsibility of caring for her daughters-in-law. The two younger women, along with Naomi, struggled to pull their lives back together. They consoled one another, worked together, and shared with one another.

Life in Moab, however, was not the same for Naomi without her husband and sons. The sun did not shine as brightly for her there anymore, and she began to think about home. She thought about the rolling hills and fertile fields of Palestine. She thought about Bethlehem with its familiar sounds and smells. Having lost her husband and sons, Naomi began to think about her own death. The thought of being buried in Moab, away from her home and kindred, did not set well with her spirit. Thus, Naomi decided to return home.

Being a fair person, she understood that she had no right to take her daughters-in-law away from their homeland. Therefore, she told them to return to their parents' homes. At first they refused to leave her, and the three of them started out for the land of Judah. As they neared the border, Naomi again spoke to them about returning to their parents' homes. She told them that she had nothing to offer them and that it grieved her to have their futures linked with her misfortunes. She reminded them that they were still young enough to have productive lives. Orpah, with much regret, turned back, but Ruth clung to Naomi. It was then that Ruth made her classic declaration of love, which has lived through the ages as one of the most beautiful expressions of devotion that has ever been uttered. She said:

> "Entreat me not to leave you or to return from following you; for where you go I will go, and where you lodge I will lodge; your people shall be my people, and your God my God; where you die I will die, and there will I be buried. May the LORD do so to me and more also if even death parts me from you" (Ruth 1: 16–17).

When Naomi saw Ruth's sincerity and determination, she remonstrated no more, and the two of them continued their journey to Bethlehem. Upon their arrival, those who remembered Naomi were stunned by her return and the change that the years and her sorrow had made upon her. Thus, they asked, "Is this Naomi?" To which she replied, "Do not call me Naomi, call me Mara, for the Almighty has dealt very bitterly with me. I went away full, and the LORD has brought me back empty. Why call me Naomi, when the LORD has afflicted me and the Almighty has brought calamity upon me?"(Ruth 1:20–21).

The name "Naomi" means "my joy," "my bliss," or the "pleasantness of Yahweh or God," and is suggestive of all that is charming, agreeable, and attractive. The term "Mara," on the other hand, means "bitter." Thus, when Naomi said, "Call me Mara," she was saying, "Why call me joyful when life has dealt harshly with me? Call me bitter because such has been my lot, my sorrow, my heartache, and my many burdens."

We all feel like Naomi sometimes. We wonder why life has treated us so harshly. With all of the healthy people we know, why are we sick? With all the happy marriages and families we know, why does our homelife have to be in turmoil? Why can't we have a peaceful home and marriage? With all of the responsible and faithful men and women we know or have met, why did we have to end up with the ones we have? With all the understanding and open-minded parents we have observed, why do ours have to be so overbearing and set in their ways? With all of the obedient children we know who have made their parents proud, why did the Lord give us such rebellious offspring who bring us so much grief? With all the evil people we know, why did the Lord have to visit our home and take our companion, our parent, our child, our sister or brother, our favorite uncle or aunt? Why did the Lord take our good friend? Why did misfortune strike us? Why did that accident happen to us? Why did tragedy visit us? Sometimes, like Naomi, we all feel like saying, "Call me Mara, for the Almighty has dealt very bitterly with me."

However, in the midst of our sorrow, let us never forget that God never leaves us without a Comforter; we are never left without a way out. In the midst of our bitterness there is sweetness; inherent in every problem there is a solution. We may not see it, but it's there. We may not want to accept the way that God has prepared for our deliverance, but it's there nevertheless. No one's life is ever totally bitter. Therefore, when life seems bitter, look for the sweetness. When the night is darkest, look for the moon; and if the moon is hidden, look for the stars. And if there are no stars to be seen, then wait in the darkness for the coming dawn. For " . . . weeping may endure for a night, but joy cometh in the morning" (Psalms 30:5, KJV).

Even as she spoke about life's bitterness, Naomi leaned

upon the arm of sweet Ruth. Naomi's life was not totally bitter because the Lord had given her sweet Ruth. When we feel alone and forsaken, we need to look for the sweet Ruths in our lives. God has put them there for us. We may not recognize them because we have selected our own Ruths. The Ruths that we chose may leave us when we need them most, but the Ruths that God has chosen for us will stay with us until the end. So when we feel lonely, instead of asking why God has dealt so harshly with us, maybe we should pray, "Lord, show me the Ruth that you have placed in my life to help change my bitterness into sweetness."

If God gives us a Ruth, let's treat her right. If God gives us good parents who constantly pray for us and who have our best interests at heart, even before their own, let's treat them right. If God has given us good companions, let's treat them right. Others may look more flashy or exciting, but they are not the Ruths that God has selected for us. We ought never mistreat our Ruths because we have our eyes on others. Those who mistreat one Ruth will mistreat another; those who will lie to one Ruth will lie to another. If God has given us good friends, we should never start taking them for granted or using them. We ought never be disloyal to Ruths who have shown themselves to be friends because we're trying to fit in with a new crowd. If God has given us Ruths, let's treat them right, because they may be the sources of our blessings.

Naomi and Ruth arrived in Bethlehem at harvest time. As they journeyed to Bethlehem, they wondered how they were going to eat. But when they arrived, they discovered that eating would not be a problem. During the season of harvest there was an abundance of grain. After the reapers went through the fields to gather the grain, the poor were allowed to pick the gleanings that were left. Since Naomi was too old to work, Ruth volunteered to glean in one of the fields. She selected a field that belonged to a wealthy man named Boaz. Ruth didn't know it, but Boaz was a kinsman of Naomi's deceased husband. Boaz happened to be passing through the fields and noticed Ruth and inquired about her. A working woman in the field was probably not her most attractive self, yet Boaz noticed her. God's children stand out wherever they are. Whether in a prison like Joseph or in a reed basket floating down the Nile River like baby Moses or in a crowd like Saul, first king of Israel, or in a field like Ruth, God's children have a way of standing out wherever they are. We don't have to wear outlandish clothing or speak in strange tongues. We don't have to exhibit strange behavior. If we are children of God, there will be something about our character that will cause others to notice us.

Boaz asked Ruth to glean only in his fields and instructed her to stay close to the other women so that no harm would come to her. Gleaning in the fields could be dangerous because sometimes the young men who were the reapers would take advantage of unsuspecting females who were all alone. Boaz told his men not to bother her and to leave a little extra grain for her to find. When thirsty, Ruth was allowed to drink with the reapers. When Ruth asked Boaz why he was being so nice to her, he replied that he had heard how kind she had been to her mother-in-law. He hoped that the Lord would bless her for her goodness.

A courtship ensued between Ruth and Boaz, with some behind-the-scenes direction from Naomi. Those who are young are called because they are strong; those who are old are needed because they know the way. Sweet Ruth was young enough and industrious enough to go to the field; she had enough character to attract Boaz's attention. But when she left the field, she had to rely on her mother's-in-law advice because Naomi knew the way to Boaz's heart. Ruth and Boaz were soon married, and in time a son was born to them. Naomi was asked to nurse their son. This same Naomi who came to Bethlehem saying, "Call me Mara because my life has been bitter"—this same Naomi who didn't know where she would live or how she would eat—ended up living in the home of one of the richest men in Bethlehem. The same women who asked, "Is this Naomi?" came to her with a hymn of praise. For the child was named Obed, which means "a son has been born to Naomi." Naomi thought her life was over, but she discovered that it was just beginning when she reached Bethlehem.

God is still able to turn bitterness into sweetness and emptiness into fullness. Our lives can also begin again. Long after Naomi, Ruth, Boaz, and their son, Obed, were dead and gone, in the fields of Bethlehem some shepherds were watching their flocks by night.

> And an angel of the Lord appeared to them, and the glory of the Lord shone about them, and they were filled with fear. [But] the angel said to them, "Be not afraid; for behold, I bring you good news of a great joy which will come to all the people; for to you is born this day in the city of David a Savior, who is Christ the Lord. And this will be a sign for you: you will find a babe wrapped in swaddling cloths and lying in a manger." And suddenly there was with the angel a multitude of the heavenly host praising God and saying,
>
> > "Glory to God in the highest,
> > and on earth peace among men with whom he is
> >   pleased!"
> > —Luke 2:9-14

Bitterness can be turned into sweetness, for

> > The people who walked in darkness
> >   have seen a great light;
> > those who dwelt in a land of deep darkness,
> >   on them light has shined.
> > —Isaiah 9:2

12

The Friend: Jonathan

Text: 1 Samuel 23:16

Those who are successful soon discover that they are the recipients of unwarranted jealousy and resentment. They are often resented by those whom they out-perform. Sometimes they are resented by their peers or even their social, educational, financial, or professional superiors. This was the painful lesson that David learned in his stormy relationship with the erratic King Saul.

When David and Saul first met, Saul was happy to have the young, agile, and courageous shepherd boy from the plains of Bethlehem in his life and on his side. Saul was in a crisis and did not know what he would do. As commander in chief of the armies of Israel, Saul had reached a stalemate in a war with the Philistines, and the future of God's people hung precariously in the balance. For forty days Goliath, the Philistine warrior giant, had challenged the armies of Israel to send someone to fight him. If Israel's soldier was victorious, the Philistines would serve Israel as slaves. But if Goliath won, Israel would serve the Philistines. Young David, who had been sent by his father to check on his brothers, who were soldiers in the Israelite army, volunteered for the task. To everyone's surprise, David felled the giant and was victorious in what everyone thought was a suicide assignment.

When David defeated Goliath, he became a national hero. A grateful Saul made him a resident of the palace, and David soon became one of the king's leading warriors. Saul even named him commander of his fighting men. While living in Saul's palace, David made another significant relationship. He met Jonathan, Saul's son and heir to the throne. If there is such a phenomenon as friendship or love at first sight, then such occurred between Jonathan and David. According to the Scriptures:

> . . . the soul of Jonathan was knit to the soul of David, and Jonathan loved him as his own soul. . . . Then Jonathan made a covenant with David, because he loved him as his own soul. And Jonathan stripped himself of the robe that was upon him, and gave it to David, and his armor, and even his sword and his bow and his girdle" (1 Samuel 18: 1,3–4).

Life was going well for David in the palace of Saul. He was loved by both the king and his son; he was respected by the men he commanded; and God was blessing him with victory in his battles. David was virtually a walking success story. However, in the midst of his good fortune, while he was riding the crest of national popularity, an innocent remark was made that was perceived the wrong way. This occurrence caused David's happy and secure world to begin unraveling at the seams. Between nations, individuals, corporations, and even churches, more trouble has erupted, more misunderstanding has arisen, and more confusion has been engendered by innocent remarks being interpreted the wrong way.

As David was returning from one of his military campaigns, some of the young women who greeted him began to chant, "Saul has slain his thousands, and David his ten thousands." When King Saul heard this innocent rhyme, resentment and jealousy began to fester in a heart that formerly had been full of admiration, praise, and thanksgiving. Saul muttered to himself, "They have ascribed to David ten thousands, and to me they have ascribed thousands; and what more can he have but the kingdom?" (1 Samuel 18:8).

Saul began to eye David with suspicion from that day forward.

Once jealousy and resentment are aroused and suspicion begins to build, peaceful relations cannot continue, and confrontation is inevitable. Once jealously is aroused and suspicion sets in, admiration turns to fear, love to hate, praise to criticism, support to undermining, and affection to attack. Thus, one day while David sang to Saul to soothe his troubled spirit, the insanely jealous king flew into a rage and tried to pin David to the wall with a spear. David fled the wrath of the king, gathered a few loyal men, and became a fugitive. David the warrior became David the hunted. David the national hero became David the anathema. David the king's armorbearer became David the king's enemy.

However, during all of David's trouble with Saul, Jonathan remained true to his friend. Some of David's comrades and peers who had sung his praises when he was a rising star at the palace turned against him when it was no longer politically expedient to share friendship with him. Some of those who had fought by David's side and with whom he had laughed and joked and with whom he had broken bread and shared a common lifestyle at the palace—these same people spurned him when he was no longer in the good graces of the king. But throughout all of David's trouble with Saul, Jonathan remained true to his friend.

Once during that period in which David was an outlaw, Keilah, one of the villages of Israel, was attacked by the Philistines, and the people of the town called upon David to help them. Before making a decision to become embroiled in a fight, David asked the Lord what he should do and was instructed to rescue the citizens of the village. When news reached Saul that David and his men were at Keilah, the king gathered his fighting forces and prepared to attack David. Although David had rescued one of the villages of Israel from the hands of the Philistines, Saul nevertheless decided to war against him. Once Satan afflicts us with jealously and suspicion, we lose our sense of reason and good judgment. We forget who our real foes are, and we start fighting our friends. We are unable to appreciate the help that friends and allies are giving, and we strike out at our supporters with a vehemence that ought be reserved for the real enemies of the people of God.

When David learned that Saul was preparing to come to Keilah to attack him and his men, he again sought guidance from God. He asked if the people of the town, whom he had rescued, could be counted on to be loyal to their deliverer, or if they would turn him over to Saul. The Lord told David that those whom he had helped would surrender him to the king; those whom he had delivered in their hour of need would betray him in his hour of peril. David fled Keilah and hid in the wilderness. David must have had his moments of discouragement as a fugitive. Not once but twice those to whom he had been loyal, those whose battles he had fought, those for whom he had risked his own life, had turned against him. Saul had driven him out of his presence because of insecurity, and the people of Keilah because of their ingratitude.

Through all of David's trials, however, Jonathan remained true to his friend. Jonathan sought David and came to him in the wilderness. Acquaintances may inquire about us, but a true friend, if there is any way possible, will come to see about us. True friends are not content to receive second-hand reports about our condition. True friends are not satisfied until they can lay eyes upon us for themselves.

Jonathan, unlike Saul, was able to find David. We can't hide from our friends; they can find us when no one else can. We may pretend that everything is all right and succeed in hiding our hurt from others. But we cannot hide our true feelings from true friends; they know when we are in the wilderness. They know when we are hurting, and sometimes they know where we are hurting. No matter how much we smile and protest that all is well, true friends will know otherwise. They may not always know what the problem is, but they will know that something is wrong. They know when we are in the midst of a wilderness experience.

Jonathan was David's friend, and thus he visited him in the wilderness. He could have sent David a message, but there are some tidings that only a friend can bring. A third party may be able to deliver the words, but that person cannot carry the passion of a friend. Jonathan could have sent David some money. While money is important, there are some things that money cannot do. Money can't listen when we need to pour out our souls. Money can't give us the warmth of human companionship. Money can't bow on its knees and pray with and for us. Money cannot speak the word of comfort or correction that we may need to hear.

Jonathan visited David in the wilderness and strengthened his hand in the Lord. Jonathan was a true friend, not simply because he came to David, but also because he came with the right spirit and the right message. He went to help rather than hinder, to encourage rather than discourage. He didn't add to David's self-pity by telling him that he had received a bad break. He didn't add to David's bitterness by rehashing and recounting all the inequities that David had received. He didn't add to David's misery, as did the friends of Job, by accusing him of unrighteousness. Jonathan didn't come with a lot of idle chatter and gossip regarding the political intrigues of those around Saul. Jonathan didn't come with physical weapons to help David wage war. To do so would have been an act of betrayal of his father. Jonathan was an honorable person, and thus his visit had integrity, even though his father would not have approved of it. Jonathan didn't visit David to betray his father; Jonathan visited David to encourage his friend. Jonathan visited David and strengthened his hand in God.

Blessed is the individual who has friends who know how to strengthen his or her hand, not in the weapons of this world, but in God. Blessed is the person whose friends do more than engage in frivolous conversation, but who also know how to encourage us to trust in God. We are blessed when we have friends who can talk to us about the goodness, faithfulness, power, and promises of God. When we are feeling useless and defeated, we are indeed blessed to have friends' who can remind us that Jesus saves to the utmost. When we begin to doubt ourselves, we are blessed to have friends who can strengthen us in faith, hope, courage, and patience.

The words of Jonathan reminded David that the anointing he received from the prophet Samuel was still good and that the word which was given to him as he knelt in his father's house was still true. Jonathan told him: "Fear not; for the hand of Saul my father shall not find you; you shall be king over Israel, and I shall be next to you; Saul my father also knows this" (1 Samuel 23: 17). Jonathan was saying to David, "You may be down now, but you shall rise again. My father, the king, may have a long reach, but there is an arm that's longer than his. His power may be great, but there is a Power greater than his. You shall reign as king, and even my father, in spite of all that he is doing, recognizes this truth."

Jonathan had to be a big person to make this statement without either bitterness or envy. After all, as Saul's son, Jonathan was the heir to the throne of Israel. In order to say what he did, Jonathan had to be willing to forfeit what might have come to him. He had to be willing to give up in order that his friend might gain. Jonathan had to be willing to sacrifice his claim to the throne so that God's will would be done in the life of his friend. Jonathan was an unusual personality and friend. I do not know how many of David's own brothers and family visited him in the wilderness, but I know that Jonathan did. Jonathan was truly "a friend who sticks closer than a brother" (Proverbs 18: 24).

Yet as good a friend as Jonathan was, as good as some of the Jonathans in our own lives may be, we have another Friend who far surpasses any Jonathan that we may know. We have another Friend who not only sticks closer than a brother but who is nearer than breath and closer than hands and feet. We have another Friend who sacrificed all in order that we might gain. Paul wrote: "For you know the grace of our Lord Jesus Christ, that though he was rich, yet for your sake he became poor, so that by his poverty you might become rich" (2 Corinthians 8:9). This Friend gave up a throne so that we might sit on one. He uncrowned himself so that we might receive a crown of glory that fades not away. He gave up the garments of eternity for a season that we might forever dwell in heavenly places.

We have a Friend who also visited in the wilderness. When Satan and sin forced us into hiding, our Friend visited us and strengthened our hand in God. Christmas is the observance of the coming of our Friend into the wilderness. Holy Communion is the remembrance of our Friend's sacrifice for us, and Easter is the celebration of our Friend's victory.

After Jonathan strengthened David's hand in the wilderness, he went back home. While David stayed in the wilderness, he had a different spirit; he could endure the wilderness a little better because his hand had been strengthened in God by his friend.

One day, after his mission was accomplished, our Friend stepped on a cloud and went back home. He left us in the wilderness with two promises—first, that he was preparing a place for us and was coming back to get us so that we could reign and be with him. Second, he promised that he would not leave us alone but would send the Holy Spirit to comfort us when we are distressed, teach us when we are confused, and empower us when we are weak. Therefore, even though we may be in the wilderness, we know that we will emerge because our hand has been strengthened in God by our Friend. We may not be as young or as experienced or as smart as others, but we're not worried because we're fighting the battles of life with a strong hand. Our hand is strong in God. One writer has said,

Many things about tomorrow, I don't seem to understand;
But I know who holds tomorrow, And I know who holds my hand.[1]

13

This Is My Story: Luke

Text: Luke I:1-4

I once tried to preach a sermon entitled "The Importance of Unimportant People." The thesis of that sermon was that persons looked upon as the least made significant contributions to the ministry of Jesus and that so-called unimportant people still make important contributions to the work of the kingdom. If anyone represents the truth of this statement, Luke does. Unlike Matthew, Luke was not one of the original twelve disciples called by Jesus. Unlike Mark, Luke's family was not intimately involved with Jesus and the Twelve. If Paul considered himself one untimely born, Luke was even more so. Matthew could claim to have been personally called by Jesus. Mark could claim to have known Jesus personally. Paul could claim to have had a vision of the resurrected and exalted Christ. Luke claimed none of those things. Luke's main link to the Jesus Christ proclaimed by the apostles was Paul, the one whose own apostleship was challenged by some.

Although theories abound as to when or how or where or the circumstances under which Paul and Luke met, the consensus is that the two of them were very close. In the passages in the epistles to the Colossians and Philemon where Mark is mentioned as being present, Luke is mentioned as being there also. It is in the Colossians passage that Paul refers to Luke as "the beloved physician." In Second Timothy where Paul requests Timothy to bring Mark, he states that only Luke is with him. For two years he was Paul's companion in imprisonment in Caesarea. Luke was also with Paul during many of his travels. When one reads the book of Acts, also written by Luke, one notes that the narratives are generally written in the third person. Luke reports on what "they" did or what happened to "them." However, in certain passages the first person is used. The author talks about what "we" did or what happened to "us." The "we" passages indicate that the author at those points was not relying on the reports of others, but on his own experience as he traveled with Paul to preach the risen Christ. The twin books of Luke and Acts, then, reflect the Pauline influence in the same way that the Gospel of Mark mirrors the influence of Peter.

One of the major Pauline themes that we see reflected in Luke-Acts is the assertion of the universal character of the gospel. Matthew, in the opinion of some, was primarily writing to a Jewish audience and was most interested in demonstrating that Jesus was the promised Messiah according to the Hebrew Scriptures. Luke, however, was writing to the Gentiles and was primarily interested in presenting Jesus not only as the Savior in terms of the Hebrew mind-set but also as the Savior of the world. Matthew constantly quoted the Old Testament, but Luke seldom did. In Luke, Calvary is not called by its Hebrew name, Golgotha, but by its Greek name, Kranion (which is translated "The Skull"). Luke never used the term "Rabbi" in referring to Jesus, but always used the Greek term meaning Master. When Matthew traced the descent or genealogy of Jesus, he stopped with Abraham, the father of faith for the Jews. Luke, on the other hand, traced the genealogy of Jesus back to Adam, the father of the human race. Theophilus, the person to whom both Luke and Acts were addressed, was a Gentile. Luke began his gospel by saying to him:

"Inasmuch as many have undertaken to compile a narrative of the things which have been accomplished among us, just as they were delivered to us by those who from the beginning were eyewitnesses and ministers of the word, it seemed good to me also, having followed all things closely for some time past, to write an orderly account for you, most excellent Theophilus, that you may know the truth concerning the things of which you have been informed" (Luke 1:1–4).

Theophilus means "dear to God," and the form of address "your excellency" suggests that he held some sort of rank or office in one of the provinces of the empire. The very person to whom the Gospel is addressed says that all of God's children are precious. There have always been persons who believed that their election for service meant that God was their personal property and exclusive possession. God, however, does not belong to any one of us; rather, every one of us belongs to God. There are so many of us who act and pray as if God belongs only to us. We expect God to bless only those whom we like—those, more often than not, who are just like us. We expect God to dislike and punish those whom we dislike. If anything bad happens to them, we believe that God is punishing them for something they did to us. But where would we be if God punished us for the wrong we've done to others? No, God is not the exclusive possession of any one person, nation, race, class, or religion. People everywhere, including those we don't like and those who don't like us and those who are different from us, are like Theophilus—"dear to God" and precious in God's sight because all of us bear the stamp of the divine image.

It is unlikely that Theophilus was a Christian since if that had been the case, Luke would have addressed him as "brother" rather than "most excellent." We as Christians these days have become enamored with our titles. We are "Doctor," "Reverend," "Steward," "Trustee," "President," or "Chairperson." If we want some good Christians and "church pillars" to become upset and stop speaking to us, all we have to do is get their titles wrong. However, in the early church the saints were known to one another as "Brother" and "Sister." When Ananias was sent to Saul after his Damascus Road experience, Ananias had his reservations about going to Paul. However, after the Spirit of the Lord directed him to do so, Ananias addressed this new bewildered convert by saying, "Brother Saul . . . " (Acts 9:17b).

Even in the church of my childhood, people were addressed as "Brother" and "Sister," "Mother" and "Father," "Uncle" and "Aunt." Those forms of address indicated that the children of God considered themselves to be part of the same family and bespoke of a kind of closeness that can never be attained through titles. Families are bound together by blood, and in this instance of the church family, we are talking about he blood of Jesus. We expect more loyalty and commitment, more concern and caring, more patience and tolerance from persons we know as family than from those we know by their titles. And maybe, for us to truly become the family of God, we need to forget some of our titles and start referring to each other again as "Brother" and "Sister."

Luke did not disregard the works of others, but he recognized that as the church continued to grow and the kingdom of God continued to expand and acquired a newer and broader audience, its message needed to be stated in language and concepts that would make sense to those who were hearing it. All of us love to tell and hear the old gospel story, but we want that story told in such a way that we can understand it, so that it speaks to our needs, answers our questions, and can be applied to our lives. The worst thing the church can do is to tell the same old story the same old way, without being aware of changing times and differing circumstances and using the same old words and worn-out clichés that have lost their meaning and fire. What is most important is not a particular word but the God to whom that word points and the reality which that word struggles to describe

Thus Luke said, "Others before me, such as my good friend and colleague John Mark, as well as our senior Matthew, among others, have already compiled narratives of the things accomplished among us. Those accounts have relied upon the testimonies of those who were the earliest followers and eyewitnesses of those events. However, it seemed like a good idea that since I had done my research and am a witness to some things, I would update the record and give another account of the same story. Therefore, most excellent Theophilus, I have pulled together some of the various narratives along with my own insights and am presenting the gospel story in an orderly fashion that you might understand more clearly the truth you have been told about and instructed in."

The gospel story that Luke set forth to Theophilus is that of a Savior who came for all people. All four Gospel writers quoted from Isaiah 10 when they gave the message of John the Baptist: "Prepare the way of the Lord, make his paths straight" (see Matthew 3:3; Mark 1:3; Luke 3:4; John 1:23), but only Luke continues the quotation to its triumphant conclusion: "and all flesh shall see the salvation of God" (Luke 3:6). The prophet Simeon, when he held the infant, according to Luke, declared that he would be "a light for revelation to the Gentiles" as well as "glory" for the people of Israel (Luke 1:32). According to Matthew, Jesus claimed to be sent only to the lost sheep of Israel. In Matthew 10:5, when Jesus sent the disciples out to preach, he told them to go to neither the Samaritans nor the Gentiles. However, when we read Luke, we see Jesus reminding his listeners that Elijah had not been sent to the widows of Israel, but to Zarephath in Sidon, and that Elisha did not cleanse the many lepers in Israel, but only Naaman the Syrian. The hero of Jesus' parable about one who dared to give a helping hand to a fallen stranger was not the busy priest or pious Levite, but, according to Luke, it was the good Samaritan. In Luke, when ten lepers were cleansed, the only one who returned to express thanks to Jesus was the Samaritan.

Luke's Gospel has been called the "Gospel of the Underdog" because it shows a special sensitivity to the least, the lost, the poor, and those who are often overlooked. Thus, in the Magnificat found in Luke, Mary declares that

> "[God] has put down the mighty from their thrones
> and exalted those of low degreee;
> [God] has filled the hungry with good things,
> and the rich he has sent empty away."
>
> —Luke 1:52–53

In Luke, Jesus describes his ministry in terms of his commitment to those whom society is inclined to forget. In one of the few Old Testament passages found in Luke, yet consistent with the Jesus who is portrayed there, our Lord quotes Isaiah saying,

> "The Spirit of the Lord is upon me,
> because he has anointed me to preach good news to the poor.
> He has sent me to proclaim release to the captives
> and recovering of sight to the blind,
> to set at liberty those who are oppressed,
> to proclaim the acceptable year of the Lord."
>
> —Luke 4:18–19

Only in Luke do we find the parable of the rich man and Lazarus, the poor man, and the parable of the rich fool. Matthew said, "Blessed are the poor in spirit" (Matthew 5:3), but Luke said, "Blessed are you poor, for yours is the kingdom of God" (Luke 6:20).

The Jesus we meet in Luke is one who was sensitive to outcasts. In ancient Palestine, Jewish males thanked God that they were not born "a Gentile, a slave, or a woman." But women hold a special place in Luke's Gospel, and Jesus is seen as being sensitive to them. The birth narrative is told from Mary's point of view. It is in Luke that we read of Elizabeth, mother of John the Baptist, and the prophetess Anna. It is in Luke that we read of the widow of Nain and of the woman who anointed Jesus' feet in the house of Simon the Pharisee. It is Luke who makes vivid the picture of Mary and Martha and Mary Magdalene. It is in Luke that we discover that the only group that Jesus spoke to on his way to Calvary was a group of women who stood by the side of the road, openly weeping while the men were hiding in shame.

The Jesus of Luke is the friend of outcasts and sinners. Only Luke tells the parable of the self-righteous Pharisee and the despised tax gatherer. Only Luke tells the story of Jesus' friendship with Zacchaeus, the tax collector. Only Luke tells us that a dying thief on the cross was granted entrance into paradise. Only Luke tells the story of a prodigal son, who after disgracing himself was received with open arms by a loving and forgiving father.

An old lady once said to me, "Before you can really tell the story, you have to go through the experience." If Luke could tell the story of a God who was no respecter of persons, of a love that knew no barriers or bounds, of a gospel that was meant for everyone, and a salvation that was available to all, it was because he had gone through the experience of discovering that the Jesus story did not belong only to Matthew or Mark or Paul, but that it was his story also.

Luke is unique among the New Testament writers in that he was a Gentile, while all of the others were Jews. Because he was not Jewish and most of the earliest Christians were, there were probably some, bound by their own prejudice, who tried to look down on Luke. But Luke did not let the snubs and feelings of others take his joy and stop him from making his own witness. He knew that Jesus died and rose for him. He knew that Jesus had accepted him as one of his own, and therefore the story of others became his story also. He wrote his own narrative. Luke-Acts makes up approximately one-fourth of the New Testament and is the largest block of writing by a single author found in the New Testament, including the thirteen Pauline letters. And it was written by a Gentile, an outcast, who discovered that this same Jesus who came to save others came to save him also.

A young Christian once told me, "I don't just talk about God and Jesus anymore; rather, I talk about my God and my Jesus." That's what salvation is—when we discover that the same God who brought others, the same Jesus who saved others, the same Holy Spirit who empowers others, belongs to each of us. Jesus is not only the preacher's Savior or the church members' Savior, or our mother's and father's Savior, but our Saviour, too. And, because he's our Savior, too, like Luke, we can have our own story to tell. Someone has written:

> Blessed assurance, Jesus is mine!
> O what a foretaste of glory divine!
> Heir of salvation, purchase of God,
> Born of His Spirit, washed in His blood.
>
> This is my story, this is my song,
> Praising my Savior all the day long;
> This is my story, this is my song,
> Praising my Savior all the day long.[1]

[1]Words by Fanny J. Crosby.

14

From Mess to Miracle: Tamar

A Sermon for Mother's Day[1]

Texts: Genesis 38:24–28 and Matthew 1:1–6:16

This message has one key point. In the course of delivering it, a number of things will be said that, hopefully, will be instructive, encouraging, and inspirational. However, underlying all that is said will be one major theme. It is a theme that has been stated over and over again from the pulpit. It is a theme that we meet over and over again as we read the Scriptures. It is one that fascinates me and moves me and causes me to marvel at the wonder-working power of God as well as the intricate design of the providential tapestry of human destiny. I never cease to be amazed at how God can turn crises into heaven's opportunities or at how God can bring victory out of defeat, redemption out of situations that seem to be unsalvageable, or good out of evil. In other words, this message is intended to be the celebration of the fact that God is able to make a miracle out of a mess.

We all know that God is able to bring good out of evil and a miracle out of a mess when we read the story of Joseph, the son of Jacob who was sold by his brothers into slavery, but who, in the end, fed his brothers when they came to Egypt begging bread. Joseph was able to feed them because

[1]The integrity of the craft mandates that I recognize Rev. T. Larry Kirkland, pastor of Brookins A.M.E. Church of Los Angeles, Cal., for giving me the idea for this sermon.

the mysterious ways of God had brought him into power as prime minister of Egypt. Chapters 37 through 50 in the Book of Genesis tell the Joseph story. When we observe the betrayal and deceit of Joseph's brothers, there is mess enough among the sons of Jacob. However, in chapter 38 there is another messy situation that outranks even the Joseph story in terms of its shame. A number of us who read the Scriptures are so preoccupied with the Joseph story that we sometimes read over or rush past the messy situation found in chapter 38.

This messy situation begins with the marriage of Judah, the fourth son of Jacob, to a Canaanite woman whose name was Shua. From this union three sons were born: Er, which means "watcher"; Onan, which means "strength"; and Shelah, which means "peace." When Er, the eldest son, became of age, Judah chose for him a wife named Tamar. Er, however, was a very wicked young man. He was so wicked that, according to the Scriptures, the Lord slew him.

These days when we observe the exploitation of young children in pornographic pictures and in prostitution, when we see elementary school children being used to push and deal in drugs, we take note of the fact that it doesn't take a long time for a young life to fall under the rule of Satan and evil. Satan can strip a young life of its innocence at an earlier age than we care to imagine. When I look at the early ages that children are involved in serious crime, including murder, I'm inclined to believe that parents must begin praying for their children before they are born, even while they are being carried in the womb. I'm convinced that parents cannot begin too early to train up their children in the ways that they should go.

Not every death of a young man or woman is the result of sin or wickedness, but Er's was. The levirate law of marriage, which was the custom of that time, stated that when a man died childless, his next eldest brother was to perform the duty of a husband to his widow. Any children resulting from such a union would be regarded as the offspring of the deceased brother. In this way his name would continue to live, and his property would have an heir. When Er died, Judah instructed Onan, his second son, to go in to Tamar, his brother's widow, that offspring might be given to his brother. However, since Onan knew that any children born to him and Tamar would not be his, he did not totally fulfill his obligations. The Lord was not pleased with his actions or his attitude, so according to the Scriptures, Onan was slain also.

Having only one son left—Shelah, who was not of marriageable age—Judah instructed Tamar to remain a widow in his household until Shelah became of age. As time passed, however, she noticed that Shelah, the youngest son, had become of age and that Judah had not kept his promise to her. She had been a faithful widow and had kept herself pure, and was feeling betrayed. She suspected that Judah had no intention of keeping his word and giving her his youngest son to wed. In the course of time, the wife of Judah died. After the appropriate period of mourning, he left home to shear the sheep. When Tamar heard that Judah was leaving home, she decided to take matters into her own hands. She decided to strike out at Judah at a time when he was most vulnerable, when he had been recently bereft of the companionship that he had had for years. She discarded her mourning attire and devised a scheme to seduce her father-in-law.

Covering her face, Tamar dressed up like a prostitute and stationed herself at the gates of one of the villages on the road that Judah would be traveling. Tamar may have been wronged, to be sure, but two wrongs have never produced a right. Two wrongs never produce justice, they only make a mess. In a marriage or any human relationship, whenever one person who has been wronged decides to take matters into his or her own hands by committing another wrong, the end result is never justice, but a mess. Much of the mess in churches today has developed over the years as certain members who have felt wronged have decided to help the

Lord out in righting their cause. They have taken matters into their own hands and have devised their own schemes for evening the score. Consequently, some boards, organizations, and choirs are in a state of mess. Some programs and projects are in a state of mess. The hostility between some people is great enough to send both of their souls to hell. Getting even, backbiting, internecine warfare, undercutting one another at every opportunity, being supercritical and hypersensitive, finding fault, gossiping, lying, setting traps for others, making fun of others, finding glee in the failures of others, senseless and time-consuming political games and power plays, failing to cooperate and work with one another—none of these produce justice; they only produce more mess.

Tamar sat on the side of the road with her face covered. Prostitutes in those days covered their faces. Goodness and righteousness can operate in the open, but evil and wrong often need a cloak to hide behind. Goodness and truth can openly declare, "This is how I honestly feel," or "This is my true opinion." But deceit and evil often try to cover their face by saying, "They said . . . " or "People are talking . . . " or "I heard . . . " or "Somebody told me . . . ."

When Judah saw Tamar on the side of the road with her face covered, he approached her, not knowing that he was about to enter into an illicit relationship with his daughter-in-law. He agreed to give her a young goat for her services. However, he didn't have one with him at the time. Tamar required that he leave his bracelets, seal, and staff as a pledge that he would send the kid later. Judah went in to her and went on his way. After he left, Tamar arose, went back home, and dressed again in the garments of her widowhood. Judah's servant tried to deliver the kid, but could not find the woman.

About three months later, news was brought to Judah that his daughter-in-law was pregnant. Judah, with self-righteous and hypocritical outrage, ordered that she be burned. Tamar then sent Judah's bracelets, seal, and staff to him with the message, "By the man to whom these belong I am with child." Judah was forced to admit that he had wronged his daughter-in-law by withholding his youngest son from her. As a result, he had committed incest and was the father of his own grandchildren—the twins, Perez and Zerah, who were born to Tamar.

What a mess and what a terrible shame on the family of Judah. What good could ever come from such a messy and scandalous situation? Such duplicity, betrayal, and sin causes us, even in our liberated society, to blush. This thirty-eighth chapter of Genesis is forgotten as quickly as it is mentioned. We never hear of Tamar and her children again in any of the remaining chapters in Genesis or in any of the other thirty-eight books of the Old Testament.

However, when we open the New Testament, beginning with the Gospel of Matthew, chapter 1, we read these words:

> The book of the genealogy of Jesus Christ, the son of David, the son of Abraham. Abraham was the father of Isaac, and Isaac the father of Jacob, and Jacob the father of Judah and his brothers, and Judah the father of Perez and Zerah by Tamar, and Perez the father of Hezron, and Hezron the father of Ram, and Ram the father of Amminadab, and Amminadab the father of Nahshon, and Nahshon the father of Salmon, and Salmon the father of Boaz by Rahab, and Boaz the father of Obed by Ruth, and Obed the father of Jesse, and Jesse the father of David the king. And David was the father of Solomon by the wife of Uriah . . . .

In verse 16 of the same chapter we read of a Jacob other than the one who fathered Judah. We are told that this Jacob was the father of Joseph, the husband of Mary, of whom Jesus was born who is called Christ.

According to the Scriptures, in the ninth generation after the mess between Judah and Tamar, in the same family, David, Israel's greatest king, was born. According to the Scriptures, in the tenth generation after the mess between Judah and Tamar, in the same family, Solomon, history's wisest man, was born. And, according to the same Scriptures, thirty-seven generations after the mess between Judah and Tamar, one night in Bethlehem, the city of David, Jesus, who was called Christ, God's only begotten Son, was born to a virgin named Mary, who was married to a man named Joseph, who was a direct descendant of Perez, the son of Judah and Tamar. From mess to miracle—from the mess between Judah and Tamar, to the miracle of David, Israel's greatest king; from the mess of Judah and Tamar, to the mess of David and Bathsheba, to the miracle of Solomon, history's wisest man; from the mess of Judah and Tamar, to the miracle of the birth of Jesus Christ, our Dayspring from on high. I repeat, I never cease to be amazed at how God can bring good out of evil and turn messes into miracles.

Mother's Day is a time when we lift up all womanhood. I say that we lift up all women on this day, not only those who are specifically mothers, because all women have shared in the responsibility of mothering black people. Our mothers have not only been those who have borne their own children. Our mothers have been older sisters who have raised the family when death or some other circumstances took natural mothers away. Our mothers have been grandmothers far beyond their childbearing years and aunts, some of whom never had children. Our mothers have been relatives and friends of our family who have taken children under their wings. Our mothers have been persons of compassion who served as foster parents or who accepted those with whom the major connecting link was not biology, but love. Our mothers have been teachers, some of whom didn't have their own children, but who served as role models for and taught us so much about kindness and character. Our mothers have been church ladies (not simply church women, but church ladies) who thought enough of us to work with us, correct us when we were wrong, encourage us when we were downcast, and pray for us when we didn't realize it.

Mother's Day is especially significant in the black community because of our history. Motherhood on these shores began in the messy situation of slavery. From the outset, slavery was designed to disrupt stable black family life. One-parent families became all too characteristic of our history. And more times than we care to admit, that one parent was the mother. As with Tamar, birth was often difficult, life was hard, work was grueling, sacrifices were great, pleasures were few, and rewards were scant. If any group of women had the right to consider abortion, that group was enslaved black women. If any group of women had the right to ask the question, "Why should I bring another life into the world to be a victim?" that group was oppressed black women. If any group of women had the right to be angry and cynical, that group was black women.

Yet, as I look at the history of motherhood among us, it seems that as our women bore the double cross of racism and sexism, God also gave them a double portion of patience and grace, dreams and hopes, strength and determination to make life better for their children. And today whenever we see successful black people, we are looking at miracles. Sometimes we as blacks resent others among us who do well. However all of us share the same dark and stormy history. We all share the messy legacy of slavery. Therefore, when any black person succeeds, the rest of us, rather than feeling jealous, need to say, "Thank God for the miracle." Whenever we open *Black Enterprise* and read about successful black businesses, we need to say, "Thank God for the miracle." Whenever we read *Essence* magazine and see page after page of beautiful, refined black womanhood, we should clap our hands and say, "Thank God for the miracle." Whenever we turn on the television and see black people with their own shows, we should say, "Thank God for the miracle." Whenever we see black co-stars on major network shows, we should say, "Thank God for the miracle." When we have a holiday named after Martin Luther King, Jr., we should say, "Thank God for the miracle." And anytime we see Jesse Jackson running in earnest as a serious candidate for the presidency of these United States, we should say, "Thank God for the miracle."

Whenever we go to a graduation ceremony in the blighted urban and depressed rural areas of this country and see young people and others who have come out of messy home situations receiving diplomas, we should say, "Thank God for the miracle." Thank you, Jesus, because you brought us a mighty long way. When our history is examined, it can be said of all of us:

Stony the road we trod, bitter the chastening rod,
Felt in the day when hope unborn had died;
Yet with a steady beat, have not our weary feet
Come to the place for which our fathers sighed?
We have come over a way that with tears has been watered,
We have come, treading our path through the blood of the slaughtered;
Out from the gloomy past, till now we stand at last
Where the white gleam of our bright star is cast.[2]

From mess to miracle—that's our history, and that's also the story of Jesus. He came from a mess to a miracle. See the mess on Calvary—God's own anointed, dying the death of a criminal between two thieves. What a mess! See how they hung him high and stretched him wide. What a mess! His disciples standing far off were too ashamed and too afraid to own him as Lord. What a mess! Hear his own cry of loneliness, "My God, My God, why have you forsaken me?" What a mess! See him drop his head between his shoulders and die between a sorrowing heaven and a sinning earth. What a mess! But early that third day, behold the miracle as God raised him to stoop no more, with heaven's glory draped around his shoulders and a shout of victory upon his lips, as he proclaimed, "All power is given unto me in heaven and in earth" (Matthew 28:18, KJV). What a miracle!

[2]"Lift Every Voice and Sing," words by W.B. Stevens, © Copyright Edward B. Marks Music Corporation. Used by permission.

15

Our Place or God's?: Judas

Text: Acts 1:23–25

I have been asked any number of times whether or not Judas was predestined or foreordained to betray Jesus? For if he was, he really should not be blamed for his crime and is deserving of our sympathy, since he had no choice in the matter. After all, Matthew's Gospel does say that "the Son of man goes as it is written of him, but woe to that man by whom the Son of man is betrayed! It would have been better for that man if he had not been born" (Matthew 26:24). I answer this question in two ways. First, I believe that while the death of God's anointed on behalf of sin was foreordained, I do not believe that Judas was personally predetermined to betray our Lord. Judas, for whatever reasons, made his own decision to betray Jesus. When we look at the other disciples—their weaknesses, personal ambitions, lack of understanding of Jesus' true mission, and their lack of faith—any of them were capable of choosing the betrayer's role. Yet none of the other disciples betrayed Jesus and turned him over to his enemies. Judas, then, was responsible for his act of treachery, and thus he went to his own place.

Second, I believe in the justice of God, and predestination, for me, denies God's justice. If Judas had been predestined to betray Christ, that assertion says to me that God is not just. For it means that God creates some people to be saved and others to be damned. It means that some people have the opportunity to be saved by the blood of Christ and others do not. It means that God created some people to be poor, oppressed, and degraded, while others were created to enjoy the fruits of life and tyrannize over others. A system in which God predetermines the destiny of individuals might easily mean that slavery was the effect of God's will and not the result of human sin and greed and that black people may have been created to be hewers of wood, drawers of waters, and servants of whites for all of their days, as some have claimed. It means that the white South African regime can claim divine approval of apartheid. A system in which God predetermines the destiny of individuals might easily mean that Hitler was correct in his master race theory and that he was justified in his slaughter of over five million Jews in this century.

The Scriptures tell us that "God so loved the world"—not just part of it, not just the white or black or Western part of it, not just the male part of it, but the whole world—"that he gave his only begotten Son, that whosoever"—not just Peter, James, and John, not just the people I like or my friends or those who look like me, but whosoever, including Judas—"believeth in him shall not perish, but have everlasting life" (John 3:16, KJV). Thus, whether or not we become part of the elect is as much a matter of our decision as it is God's will. When we accept Christ as our Savior and Lord of our lives, when we say yes to the doing of God's will, we become part of the elect. The Scriptures say that those who are the elect are not elected for special privileges, but for greater service and sacrifice. I believe that God has created all of us for salvation. I believe God has a place in eternity, in heaven, for all of us. I believe that the divine will is that we live eternally with God in the unity of the Son and the blessed Holy Spirit. Jesus told the disciples,

> "Let not your hearts be troubled; believe in God, believe also in me. In my Father's house are many rooms; if it were not

so, would I have told you that I go to prepare a place for you? And when I go and prepare a place for you, I will come again and will take you to myself, that where I am you may be also" (John 14:1–3).

Christ has already prepared a place of glory and honor in the presence of God for every one of us. The decision, however, as to whether or not we go to God's place or our own, is ours to make.

According to our text, Judas went to his own place, that of a betrayer, but that was not the place that Christ had intended for him. Jesus did not call Judas so that Judas could betray him. Jesus did not call Judas so that his soul could be eternally damned. That would have been a cunning plot of cruelty by a manipulating, game-playing Lord, unbefitting the character of Christ. Jesus called Judas for friendship, special revelation, and a unique fruitbearing ministry of intercession. Our Lord told his disciples,

> "No longer do I call you servants, for the servant does not know what his master is doing; but I have called you friends, for all that I have heard from my Father I have made known to you. You did not choose me, but I chose you and appointed you that you should go and bear fruit and that your fruit should abide; so that whatever you ask the Father in my name, he may give it to you" (John 15:15–16).

That was Jesus' hope for Judas as well as the other disciples. Because much would be expected from the disciples, much would be given, and they would receive a special inheritance. Jesus told them,

> "You are those who have continued with me in my trials; and I assign to you, as my Father assigned to me, a kingdom, that you may eat and drink at my table in my kingdom, and sit on thrones judging the twelve tribes of Israel" (Luke 22:28–30).

Jesus meant this for Judas as well as the others, but Judas rejected the place prepared and set aside for him and went to his own place.

Judas had to have had potential, otherwise Christ would

not have called him. He had to have had potential, otherwise he never would have held the only office in the group. Judas, as the treasurer, had the only official title or designated responsibility among the disciples. Peter may have taken charge and assumed the role of spokesman on his own. John may have been the "beloved" disciple. The two of them along with James may have had some experiences that the others didn't have. Andrew may have had seniority, but Judas, as the treasurer of the group, was the only duly authorized officer among them. If Judas had just followed through on the potential that he had shown, he would have ended in a far different place than the one he eventually reached.

Life's race, the judgments of history, and the reward of God are not given to the swift or the strong, but to the one who endures until the end. So many lives and careers start off with great promise and end in great shame. Someone has correctly observed that "[we] can never tell by the brightness of the dawn or the noontide how the evening of the day will be. The brightest sun may go down in a dark and clouded day." That's why we must be careful about saying that certain young people, certain marriages, certain ideas, and certain careers will not amount to anything. When life's final chapter is written, some who started out first end up last and the last, first. Sometimes the most promising among us go to their own place, as did Judas, while others of us, like James the Less, the disciple about whom hardly anything is known, remain faithful and go to the place prepared by Christ.

Judas went to his own place because he neglected to take full advantage of his opportunities. What a privilege it would have been to have been close enough to see Jesus' facial expressions and hear his voice when he delivered the Sermon on the Mount. Some would love to have been there when Jesus fed the five thousand with a little boy's lunch or when he raised Lazarus from the dead. Some would love to have been there on the first Palm Sunday. What a privilege

to have been present when Jesus was anointed with an alabaster flask of costly ointment, the only extravagance ever
given or received by Jesus during his life. To have been there
on that first Maundy Thursday when Jesus washed his disciples feet, to have seen him break the bread and lift the cup
and hear him say, "This is my body broken for you . . . This
is my blood shed for you," would have been such a privilege.
Judas was present on all of these occasions and had failed to
be impressed by all that he had seen or heard. Instead, he
pursued his own course, worked on his own agenda, and
ended up going to his own place.

When we fail to take advantage of life's opportunities, we
end up in a place of our own making and choosing. When
the gospel is presented to us and we fail to repent and begin
living anew, we end up going to our own place. When we
allow misunderstanding and other people or things to prevent us from receiving the Word of the Lord, we end up
going to our own place. When God's Word, righteousness,
salvation, and teaching comes to us and we close our minds
to the truth, we end up going to our own place. When the
Holy Spirit comes to us and we quench it or block it, we end
up going to our own place. When we let Sunday after Sunday go by without going to church and always offer excuses
to those who encourage us to attend, we end up going to our
own place. When we let opportunity after opportunity go
by without joining the church, we end up going to our own
place.

For betraying Jesus, Judas received a reward—thirty
pieces of silver. But he received more—he went to his own
place. Sin is a fair and generous employer; it gives more than
what is promised. Adam and Eve received the knowledge of
good and evil as promised, but they were also led from
paradise and received the death sentence—more than was
promised. Achan received the wedge of gold stolen from
Jericho, as desired, but he also received the death sentence
from Joshua—more than he desired. Elisha's servant, Gehazi
received the two talents of silver and the two changes of

garments from Namaan, whom Elisha, his master, had cured without cost. Gehazai also received leprosy—more than what he sought. David received Bathsheba, and Ahab received Naboth's vineyard, but they also received the judgment of God—more than they bargained for. Judas received his thirty pieces of silver as promised, but he also received the loneliness of a traitor's place. He received the tortured conscience that comes to one who has betrayed a trust. He received the disdain of his fellow disciples and the loathing of those who had hired him to betray his Lord and Master. The place that Judas made for himself was so distasteful that he couldn't live there, so he went out and hung himself and was buried in a potter's field.

The place that Jesus had chosen for Judas was a much higher place:

> "What no eye has seen, nor ear heard,
> nor the heart of man conceived,
> what God has prepared for those who love him."
> —1 Corinthians 2:9

When John described the throne of God, he said that seated around the throne were twenty-four elders—twelve representing the tribes of Israel and twelve representing the apostles. The place that Jesus had chosen for Judas was around the throne of God. When John described the holy city, he said that the walls of the city stood on twelve foundations on which were inscribed the names of the twelve apostles of the Lamb. That was the place Jesus had chosen for Judas. However, Judas chose to go to his own place.

It is said that when Leonardo da Vinci was painting his masterpiece "The Last Supper," he searched a long time for a model of Christ. He finally located a young man who was a choir member in one of the churches in Rome. This young man, named Pietro Bondinelli, was said to be lovely in life and features. Years passed and the painting was still unfinished. All the disciples had been painted with the exception of Judas. Leonardo da Vinci began to search for a man to pose for Judas. He wanted someone whose face had been hardened and distorted by sin. At last he found a beggar in the streets of Rome, a man whose face was so villainous that the famous painter shuddered when he looked at him. He hired the man to sit for him as he painted the face of Judas. When he was about to dismiss the man, he said to him, "I have not yet found out your name." The man said, "I am Pietro Bondinelli. I also sat for you as your model of Christ."

We can wear either the face of Judas or the face of Christ. If we are now wearing the Judas face of deceit and sin, selfishness and bitterness, guilt and shame, we can wear the Christ face of love and forgiveness, salvation and peace, freedom and joy. We can go either to our own place or the place that Jesus has prepared for us with God. My desire is to wear the face of those who belong to Christ. I want to go to a place that's higher than any here below. I want to go to a place, not of my making, a place not made with hands, but to a "city which has foundations, whose builder and maker is God" (Hebrews 11:10b). I want to go to that place set aside for me by God. If history doesn't record anything I've said and done, that's all right. I want to be able to say, like Job, " . . . my witness is in heaven, and he that vouches for me is on high" (Job 16:19). I want a higher place.

16

Living with Criticism: John the Baptist and Jesus

Center Street July 5, 1992

Text: Luke 7:33–34

If we plan to survive and live triumphantly in this world, then we had better learn to live with criticism because we surely won't be able to live without it. This fact of life ought to be clear when we read the text. The people who lived in Palestine during the first three decades of the first-century A.D. were indeed blessed. Living among them and preaching in their midst were two of the greatest religious personalities who have ever proclaimed and manifested the Word of God. Both John the Baptist and Jesus were answers to the prayers of generations of faithful believers who longed for the Messiah and the forerunner, who was conceived as a latter day Elijah and who would herald the arrival of God's anointed.

Both John the Baptist and Jesus had been consecrated to God's service from their mothers' wombs. Even their names had been divinely selected. Both sets of parents had been told by angels of the significant roles that their offspring would play in the redemption of their people. Both of their births were in a sense miraculous. John was born of Elizabeth, who had long been barren and considered incapable of conceiving children. Jesus had been born of Mary, a virgin. Both John and Jesus were raised in the traditions of their people as their parents sought to do their part in preparing their sons for the ministries to which they would one day give themselves. And in time both of them responded to the Spirit of God as that Spirit began to move within their hearts and lay claim upon their lives.

After a four-hundred-year period, during which no prophet had arisen in Israel, John the Baptist appeared like a streak of lightning and a clap of thunder in the Judaean wilderness and began to preach with such power that people throughout the land were drawn to him in droves. He closely resembled Elijah, whose role in messianic theology he fulfilled. Like Elijah, John was a somewhat eccentric, ascetic desert dweller, whose fiery words burned the consciences of those who seriously listened to him. Like Elijah, he was impatient with unrighteousness, passionate about justice, and confrontational whenever he saw sin, even the sin in the king's household. Like Elijah, he was hated by the wife of the king whom he opposed. No one was more suited for the role of Elijah than John the Baptist. No prophet was anymore dedicated, courageous, or morally upright than John the Baptist.

No one was more worthy of baptizing our Lord than John, who had to have been genuine and upright. Jesus would not have submitted himself to be baptized by an imposter. Jesus would not have allowed someone with dirty hands to pour the cleansing waters of baptism upon him. Listen to what our Lord said about John:

> "What did you go out into the wilderness to behold? A reed shaken by the wind? What then did you go out to see? A man clothed in soft clothing? Behold, those who are gorgeously appareled and live in luxury are in kings' courts. What then did you go out to see? A prophet? Yes, I tell you, and more than a prophet. This is he of whom it is written,
>
>> 'Behold, I send my messenger before thy face,
>> who shall prepare the way before thee.'
>
> I tell you, among those born of women none is greater than John . . . " (Luke 7:24–28).

134

Likewise, no life was more worthy of the approbation given to Jesus by John, "Behold, the Lamb of God, who takes away the sin of the world!" (John 1:29). No personality was better suited for the role of suffering but conquering servant than Jesus, whose unity with God the Creator was perfect and whose will was in complete accord with the salvation offered by heaven to a wayward humanity. No life manifested either God's power or love like his; no mouth spoke with divine authority like his; no hands could do what his could. No wonder when Jesus came to John to be baptized, John said that he should not be baptizing Jesus, but that Jesus should be baptizing him.

The two of them perfectly complemented each other as much in their differences as in the similarities of their commitments to righteousness, truth, and the kingdom of God. John preached judgment; Jesus preached good news. John wore camel's hair; Jesus wore a seamless robe. John baptized with water; Jesus baptized with fire. John's ministry was basically rural; much of Jesus' ministry was urban. John basically stayed in one place; Jesus went from place to place. John performed no miracles; Jesus performed many mighty miracles. John ate berries and locusts; Jesus ate the traditional food of his culture. John's lifestyle was essentially that of a hermit; Jesus was more of a social creature who went to banquets, parties, and feasts when invited. Between John the Baptist and Jesus there were enough similarities and differences to satisfy the religious quest of any sincere searcher.

No other generation was as privileged as those who lived during that time. What a choice they had—John the Baptist or Jesus. What a team to follow—John the Baptist and Jesus. Just imagine, being able to listen to the preaching of John the Baptist one day and on the next day being able to find Jesus and observe his mighty works. There were some who were attracted to Jesus and others who preferred John. There were still others who didn't like either. There were those who were not satisfied with either John or Jesus. There were those who said that John was too stiff and too strange, but who also felt that Jesus was too relaxed and too ordinary. When John the Baptist appeared, living a Spartan lifestyle in the desert and eating strange food and preaching like hell was right around the corner, people said he was crazy. When Jesus appeared, living a more urbane lifestyle and eating and drinking traditional staples of his culture, people said he was a glutton and a drunkard. If John and Jesus with all of their sincerity, commitment, and perfection, could not live without criticism, neither will we. If John and Jesus were not liked by everyone, neither will we. If John and Jesus could not satisfy everyone, neither will we. I repeat—if we are to survive and be triumphant in this life, then we had better learn to live with criticism because we surely won't be able to live without it.

When some of us are criticized, we seem to think that we are being accorded special treatment. We think that people are picking on us. However, we are not necessarily receiving any special treatment when we are being criticized—everyone receives his or her share of criticism. Special treatment would be receiving no criticism. Then we would have another problem. For receiving no criticism would mean that people did not take us seriously or think enough of us to be critical. Only those who are taken seriously or who are regarded as threats or who are the victims of jealously are criticized. Better to be taken seriously enough and regarded as important enough to be talked about than to be looked upon as so unimportant, and as such a nonentity, that people don't take the time to talk about us.

Some of the same people who didn't like John the Baptist didn't like Jesus either. In other words, like many other people, all they knew how to do was criticize. A man once remarked to a friend that he had one talent. When asked what it was, he said it was the talent to criticize. His friend replied, "I suggest that you do with that talent what the man with the one talent did in the parable told by Jesus—bury it. Criticism may be useful when mixed with other talents, but those whose only ability is to criticize might as well be buried, talent and all."

Some of us might learn the lesson once taught by a father to his overly pious son. This son had developed the habit of rising earlier than his brothers and sisters to read his Bible and pray. One morning he remarked to his father, who was also an early riser, "Look at the rest of your children lost in irreligious slumber while I alone woke to praise God." The father looked at him and said, "My son, it is better to remain asleep than to waken to criticize others."

John the Baptist and Jesus were both criticized, but they both also criticized others. Not only is everyone criticized, but everyone does some criticizing. Let's not forget that point because we are inclined to remember the criticism we've received while forgetting that which we've given out. We've all done our share of dishing it out, but we shouldn't forget that there is a time and a way to criticize. If criticism were wrong, per se, then both Jesus and John would have been at fault. John was critical of Herod's sin; Jesus was critical of the Sadducees' hypocrisy. John was critical of the unjust dealings of tax collectors and soldiers; Jesus was critical of the hardheartedness of the Pharisees. Criticism is legitimate when it condemns wrong. Criticism is also legitimate when it proposes to be helpful as a corrective and stems from a desire to build up rather than tear down. There is such a thing as "speaking the truth in love."

Thus, criticism can be constructive and a weapon in the battle against sin; it only becomes ugly when it turns into faultfinding. When neither John nor Jesus satisfies us, we're not critics; we're faultfinders. When we can never find much of anything good to say about anyone or anything, we're not critics; we're faultfinders. When no one looks right to us but us, when no one has any sense but us, we're not critics; we're faultfinders. When we can clearly identify the sawdust that's in our brothers' and sisters' eyes, but can't see the plank in our own, we're not critics, we're faultfinders and hypocrites. When we magnify every little mistake, we're not critics; we're faultfinders and liars.

A boy was once watching an artist paint a picture of a muddy river. He criticized the picture because there was so much mud. The artist told him, "You see mud in the picture, and admittedly there is lots of it. But I see beautiful colors and contrasts, beautiful harmonies, and the light around the dark." When we look at life and all we can is mud; when John is baptizing in the River Jordan and all we can see is muddy water; when Jesus is making clay to be put on blinded eyes as a means of healing and all we can see is mud—we're not critics; we're faultfinders. The question that a number of sanctimonious Christians need to ask is not whether or not we ever criticize, but what kind of critics are we? Are we the helpful or hindering kind, the constructive or the destructive kind? Are we critics with love or critics with venom? Are we truthful critics or petty faultfinders?

Since criticism will be with us always, we had better learn how to handle it, or it will handle us. We will constantly lose our tempers, give up, or leave meetings with tears in our eyes if we can't handle criticism. We will continually be discouraged if we can't handle criticism. We first handle criticism by listening. Whether we like it or not, it pays to listen to criticism, even the malicious and petty type that comes from those who don't like us. It pays to listen because they just may say something to help us. If what's said is untrue, consider the source and disregard it. If what is said is true, then take heed. Even the biggest liar in the world will tell the truth sometimes. More than one child of God has been helped by enemies who sought to destroy them. Heaven is still able to take faultfinding criticism from those who have set themselves up as our enemies and use it for our good.

Second, let us not forget that when we are criticized, we're in good company. We're in the company of Noah, who was criticized for building a boat in the desert. We're in the company of Hagar, the slave woman who was criticized for being proud. We're in the company of Moses, who was criticized for leading God's children into the wilderness. We're in the company of Elijah, who was criticized for withholding rain from the land according to the Word of God. We're in the company of Micaiah, who was criticized for not prophesying good concerning Ahab. We're in the company of Job, who was criticized because of his trouble, or Daniel, who was criticized for praying too much, or Shadrach, Meshach, and Abednego, who were criticized for refusing to bow to false images. We're in the company of John the Baptist, who was criticized for not eating and drinking. We're in the company of Jesus, who was criticized for eating and drinking too much.

We're in the company of Galileo, who was criticized for stating that the earth revolved around the sun, or Columbus, who believed that the earth was round rather than flat, or Orville and Wilbur Wright, who were criticized because they believed that man could fly. We're in the company of Richard Allen, who was criticized for building a church where black people could worship without hindrance. We're in the company of Booker T. Washington, who was criticized for teaching vocational education to blacks in Tuskegee, Alabama, or George Washington Carver, who was criticized for wasting so much time on a peanut. We're in the company of Mahalia Jackson, who was criticized for singing only religious music, or Martin Luther King, Jr., who was criticized for condemning the Vietnam war. We're in the company of Jesse Jackson, who was criticized for being a serious presidential contender and thus messing up the status quo politics. So remember, when we're criticized, we're in good company. Jesus said: "Blessed are you when [people] revile you and persecute you and utter all kinds of evil against you falsely on my account. Rejoice and be glad, for your reward is great in heaven, for so men persecuted the prophets who were before you "(Matthew 5:11–12).

Third, if we know that we are right, we don't let criticism stop us—we keep on going. Criticism followed Jesus all of his life, but he kept on doing what he knew was right. He was criticized for picking grain to feed himself on the Sabbath, but he knew that as Son of man he was Lord of the Sabbath. He was criticized for healing on the Sabbath, but he kept on lifting the lame and making withered hands whole. He was criticized for being a friend to sinners, but he received the confession of Zacchaeus as well as an act of kindness from a fallen woman. He was criticized for going to Jerusalem, but he steadfastly set his face toward Jerusalem. He was criticized for talking about a cross, but he continued to declare, "And I, when I am lifted up from the earth, will draw all men to myself" (John 12:32). He was accused of blasphemy, but he continued to forgive sins and call God his Father.

Even on the cross his enemies talked about him. They said, "He saved others; he cannot save himself . . . He trusts in God; let God deliver him now . . . "(Matthew 27:42–43). But he kept on dying until a thief found paradise. He kept on dying until he could pronounce his work finished. He kept on dying until the sun went down, the earth shook, and the Holy of Holies in the temple was uncovered. He kept on dying until your sins and my sins were washed away. Because he kept dying, despite criticism, God gave him the victory and raised his name higher than any other names, so that at the name of Jesus, every knee should bow and every tongue confess that Jesus Christ is Lord over critics and faultfinders.

Your name may be cast out as evil, but keep going. You may be criticized when you give your all and do your best, but keep going. You may be falsely accused, but keep going. God will give you the victory.

ADDITIONAL WORSHIP RESOURCES PUBLISHED BY JUDSON PRESS

Best Black Sermons, William Philpot. ed. 1972. Sermons that emphasize black dignity and proclaim God's power. 0-8170-0533-1

Biblical Faith and the Black American, Latta R. Thomas. 1976. Calls upon black Americans to rediscover the liberating power of the biblical message. 0-8170-0718-0

Children's Time in Worship, Arline J. Ban. 1981. Practical ideas for involving children in corporate worship. Extensive resource section for pastors. 0-8170-0907-8

The Church in the Life of the Black Family, Wallace C. Smith. 1985. Creative ideas for a holistic program that focuses on needs in education, employment, housing, health care, and personal identity. 0-8170-1040-8

Contemporary Biblical Interpretation for Preaching, Ronald J. Allen. 1984. Uses critical exegesis in a simplified manner to develop fresh biblical interpretations for sermons. 0-8170-1002-5

Creative Programs for the Church Year, Malcolm G. Shotwell. 1986. Focuses on personalizing the gospel message with special plans for every season. 0-8170-1102-1

Cups of Light . . . and Other Illustrations for Sermons and Devotions, Clarence W. Cranford. 1988. Two hundred illustrations for sermons and meditations.0-8170-1142-0

Dedication Services for Every Occasion, Manfred Holck. Jr., compiler. 1984. Thirty.five services for just about any special celebration. 0-8170-1033-5

God Is Faithful, Julius Richard Scruggs. 1985. Practical interpretations of great Bible truths offer help for facing personal disappointments and solving problems of social injustice. 0-8170-1060-2

God's Transforming Spirit:Black Church Renewal, Preston R. Washington. 1988. Discusses important elements of church renewal—prayer discipline, dependence on the Holy Spirit for guidance, helping members grow in discipleship, and ministry to the community. 0-8170-1129-3

Interpreting God's Word in Black Preaching, Warren H. Stewart. 1984. Five-point study of the hermeneutical process for interpreting and communicating the Word so that it will be relevant to the congregation. 0-8170-1021-1

Listening on Sunday for Sharing on Monday, William D. Thompson. 1983. How the preacher and the listening congregation can become a dynamic partnership for spreading the message of God's healing power. 0-8170-1000-9

Litanies for All Occasions, Garth R. House. 1989. Scripture-inspired litanies that allow the pastor and congregation to join together in lifting up to God their praise, petitions, and thanks for blessings. 0-8170-1144-7

The Minister's Handbook, Orlando L. Tibbetts. 1986. Practical resources for worship services, special observances, and special occasions in members' lives.0-8170-1088-2

The Ministry of Music in the Black Church, J. Wendell Mapson. Jr. 1984. Shows how music can enhance worship. 0-8170-1057-2

Outstanding Black Sermons, J. Alfred Smith, ed. 1976. 0-8170-0664-8

Outstanding Black Sermons, Volume 2, Walter B. Hoard. ed. 1979. 0-8170-0832-2

Outstanding Black Sermons, Volume 3, Milton Owens, Jr., ed. 1982. 0-8170-0973-6

Redemption in Black Theology, Olin P. Moyd. 1979. Examines redemption as reflected in black history and folk expressions. 0-8170-0806-3

Sermon on the Mount, Clarence Jordan. 1970. An interpretation of Christ's sermon that explores today's problems. 0-8170-0501-3

Sermons from the Black Pulpit, Samuel D. Proctor and William D. Watley. 1984. Thirteen sermons that call for a renewed commitment to discipleship. 0-8170-1034-3

Sermons on Speacial Days: Preaching Through the Year in the Black Church, William D. Watley. 1987. Sixteen sermons for all celebrations of the Christian year. 0–8170-1089–0

"Somebody's Calling My Name," Wyatt Tee Walker. 1979. Detailed history of black sacred music and its relationship to social change. 0–8170-0980–9

The Star Book for Ministers, E. T. Hiscox. 1906. Contains forms and suggestions for every type of service in which a pastor is called upon to participate. 0–8170-0167–0

Steady in an Unsteady World, Stephen A. Odom. ed. 1986. Fourteen selections from the unpublished sermons of Leslie Weatherhead. Each brings a message of hope for people facing uncertain futures. 0–8170-1097–1

Telling the Story: Evangelism in Black Churches, James 0. Stallings. 1988. Challenges black Christians to recapture the power of their rich evangelistic heritage. 0–8170-1124–2

Those Preachin' Women, Ella Pearson Mitchell, ed. 1985. Fourteen sermons by black women that call Christians to develop positive attitudes and to find their identities by oneness in God. 0-8170-1073-4

Those Preaching Women, Volume 2, Ella Pearson Mitchell, ed. 1988. More sermons by black women. 0-8170-1131-5

Vision of Hope: Sermons for Community Outreach, Benjamin Greene, Jr., ed. 1988. Action-oriented sermons that offer a fresh view of the church's mandate for ministry to hurting people. 0-8170-1150-1